Joe Penhall

Blue/Orange

CW00517874

Bloomsbury Methuen Drama

An imprint of Bloomsbury Publishing Plc

B L O O M S B U R Y

LONDON · OXFORD · NEW YORK · NEW DELHI · SYDNEY

Bloomsbury Methuen Drama

An imprint of Bloomsbury Publishing Plc

Imprint previously known as Methuen Drama

50 Bedford Square	1385 Broadway
London	New York
WC1B 3DP	NY 10018
UK	USA

www.bloomsbury.com

BLOOMSBURY, METHUEN DRAMA and the Diana logo
are trademarks of Bloomsbury Publishing Plc

First published in 2000 by Methuen Publishing Limited
Revised edition published 2001
This edition published with some changes to the script 2016

Joe Penhall has asserted his right under the Copyright, Designs
and Patents Act, 1988, to be identified as authors of this work..

British Library Cataloguing-in-Publication Data
A catalogue record for this book is available from the British Library

ISBN: PB: 978-1-3500-1195-3
ePDF: 978-1-3500-1196-0
ePub: 978-1-3500-1197-7

Library of Congress Cataloging-in-Publication Data
A catalog record for this book is available from the Library of Congress

Cover design: Olivia D'Cruz

Typeset by Country Setting, Kingsdown, Kent CT14 8ES
Printed and bound by CPI Group (UK) Ltd, Croydon, CR0 4YY

Young Vic

Blue/Orange

by Joe Penhall

Blue/Orange was first performed in the Cottesloe auditorium of the Royal National Theatre, London, on 7 April 2000.

This production opened at the Young Vic, London, on 12 May 2016.

Blue/Orange

by **Joe Penhall**

Robert	**David Haig**
Christopher	**Daniel Kaluuya**
Bruce	**Luke Norris**

Direction	**Matthew Xia**
Design	**Jeremy Herbert**
Light	**Adam Silverman**
Sound	**Carolyn Downing**
Movement	**Joseph Alford**
Voice	**Emma Woodvine**
Casting	**Julia Horan CDG**
Assistant Director	**Michal Keyamo**

Production Manager	**Lloyd Thomas**
Stage Manager	**Rosina Kent**
Deputy Stage Manager	**Natasha Gooden**
Assistant Stage Manager	**Tom Leggat**
Costumer Supervisor	**Catherine Kodicek**
Lighting Operator	**Sebastian Barresi**
Sound Operator	**Amy Bramma**
Wardrobe Maintenance	**Nicki Martin-Harper**
Stage Management Placement	**Alice Bentham**

Draughting	**Nick Murray**
Set built and painted by	**Scott Fleary Productions**
Rigging by	**Rigging Team**
Lighting equipment supplied by	**Hawthorn**
Sound equipment supplied by	**Stage Sound Services**

Michal Keyamo is supported by the Jerwood Assistant Directors Program at the Young Vic.

With generous support from the Richenthal Foundation.

We would like to thank Dionne Monarch, Maudsley Hospital, English Touring Theatre, Richard Azoro, Jason McClean, Dr Neil Bremer, Daniel Gil-Lubeiro, Attle Costumiers Ltd., Sarah Frankcom and the Manchester Royal Exchange.

BIOGRAPHIES

David Haig

Robert

Theatre includes: *Guys and Dolls* (West End; nominated for the Olivier Award for Best Actor in a Musical); *Someone Who'll Watch Over Me* (Chichester); *Pressure* (as writer and performer; Chichester & Edinburgh Lyceum); *King Lear* (Theatre Royal Bath); *The Madness of George III* (West End & Theatre Royal Bath – Olivier nominated); *Yes, Prime Minister* (Chichester & West End); *Mary Poppins* (West End – Olivier nominated); *Donkey's Years* (West End – Olivier nominated); *Hitchcock Blonde*(Royal Court & West End); *My Boy Jack* (Hampstead); *Our Country's Good* (Royal Court; winner of the Olivier Award for Actor of the Year); *House and Garden* (National Theatre); *Art* (West End & Broadway).

Film includes: *Florence Foster Jenkins*; *Two Weeks Notice*; *Four Weddings and a Funeral*.

Television includes: *Penny Dreadful*; *The Thick of It*; *The Thin Blue Line*.

Writing includes: *Pressure*; *My Boy Jack* (also a television play: winner of FIPA Award for Best Screenplay); *The Good Samaritan*.

Daniel Kaluuya

Christopher

Previous Young Vic includes: *A Season in the Congo*.

Other theatre includes: *Trelawny of the Wells* (Donmar Warehouse); *Oxford Street*, *Sucker Punch* (Royal Court, winner of Critics' Circle Outstanding Newcomer and Evening Standard Editor's Award).

Film includes: *Sicario*; *Kick Ass*; *Johnny English*.

Television includes: *Skins*; *Black Mirror*; *Psychoville*; *Doctor Who*.

Writing includes: *Skins* (series 1, 2, 3); *Two of a Kind* (Hampstead).

Luke Norris

Bruce

Previous Young Vic includes: *A View from the Bridge* (also West End; winner of Olivier Award for Best Revival).

Other theatre includes: *Hamlet, As You Like It, The Gods Weep, Days of Significance* (Royal Shakespeare Company); *Orpheus Descending* (Royal Exchange); *Antigone, The Kitchen, The Habit of Art* (National Theatre); *Filumena* (Almeida); *Remembrance Day* (Royal Court); *War Horse* (NT West End); *White Boy* (Soho Theatre).

Television includes: *Poldark*; *Our World War*; *Titanic*; *Skins*; *The Inbetweeners*.

Writing includes: *Growth* (Paines Plough); *So Here We Are* (Bruntwood Prize, Royal Exchange Studio); *Hearts* (National Theatre Connections); *Goodbye to All That* (Royal Court).

Joe Penhall

is a playwright and screenwriter.

Theatre includes: *Sunny Afternoon* (Hampstead Theatre and West End; winner of the Olivier Award for Best New Musical in 2015); *Birthday, Haunted Child, Dumb Show, Pale Horse* (winner of Thames Television Best Play Award), *Some Voices* (winner of John Whiting Award, 1995, Royal Court); *Landscape with Weapon, Blue/Orange* (winner of Evening Standard Best Play Award, Olivier Award for Best New Play in 2001 and Critics' Circle Award for Best New Play in 2000, National Theatre); *The Bullet* (Donmar Warehouse); *Love and Understanding* (Bush Theatre).

Film includes: *The Road* (which premiered in competition at the Venice Film Festival 2009); *Enduring Love, Some Voices.*

Television includes: *Birthday* (winner of Prix d'Or at Biarritz FIPA Film Festival); *Moses Jones* (winner of Best Screenplay at the Roma Fiction Festival 2009); *The Long Firm* (nominated for BAFTA Award); *Blue/Orange.*

Matthew Xia

Direction

Matthew is a director, composer, journalist and DJ. In 2013 he was the recipient of the Regional Theatre Young Director Scheme bursary and appointed Director in Residence at the Liverpool Everyman and Playhouse Theatres. In the same year he won the Genesis Future Directors Award. A former Associate Director at the Theatre Royal Stratford East, he is currently Associate Artistic Director at Manchester's Royal Exchange.

Previous Young Vic includes: *Sizwe Banzi is Dead* (as director), *Blackta* (as assistant director), *The Sound of Yellow* (a Taking Part production).

Other theatre includes: *Into the Woods, Brink* (Royal Exchange, Manchester); *Scrappers, Opening Ceremony: Lights Up* (Liverpool Everyman and Playhouse); *I was looking at the ceiling and then I saw the sky, Mad Blud, The Blacks, Da Boyz, Cinderella, Aladdin* (Theatre Royal Stratford East); *Re:Definition, In His Hands* (Hackney Empire); *Abandonment* (Rich Mix); *Soyuz 40* (Theatre503); *Ruth the Divorcee and Barry the Lovesick Bee* (Lyric Hammersmith Studio); *When Chaplin Met Gandhi* (Kingsley Hall); *Wild Child* (Royal Court).

As a DJ, composer and former BBC Radio 1Xtra broadcaster he has performed as Excalibah across Europe and the UK, including at the 2012 Paralympic Opening Ceremony. Matthew is a founding member of Act for Change.

Jeremy Herbert

Design

Jeremy is an award-winning multi-media artist and stage designer. He is Associate Designer at the Young Vic.

Previous Young Vic includes: *Hamlet, The Glass Menagerie, Blackta,* and the experimental installation *Safe House* (in collaboration with Gabriella Sonabend).

Other theatre includes: *Cleansed, 4.48 Psychosis* (winner of the Barclays Award for Best Design), *The Alice Trilogy, The Lights, Thyestes, The Ugly One* (Royal Court); *Harper Regan* (Hamburg Schauspielhaus, Salzberg Festival); *The Triumph of Love; Parlour Song* (Almeida); *The Tempest, Robert Zucco, Beauty and the Beast* (Royal Shakespeare Company); *Betrayal, Sexual Perversity in Chicago, This Is Our Youth* (West End).

Opera includes: *La Bianca Notte, Death in Venice* (Hamburg Opera); *Rodelinda* (ENO/Bolshoi Theatre).

Jeremy's installations have included a full-sized walking house on Salisbury Plain created for Artangel and an immersive performance for the Ruhr Triennale. His most recent piece was presented at the London Frieze Art Fair 2015. He is currently working with musician PJ Harvey.

Adam Silverman

Light

Adam works as a lighting designer across opera, theatre and dance.

Previous Young Vic includes: *Hamlet, 'Tis Pity She's a Whore, Three Musketeers, Beauty and the Beast, The Nativity.*

Theatre includes: *Ballyturk, Misterman, Dido Queen of Carthage* (National Theatre); *The Glass Menagerie* (Toneelgroep Amsterdam); *Urinetown* (St James Theatre); *Macbeth* (Trafalgar Studios); *This Is Our Youth* (Garrick); *My Fair Lady* (Théâtre du Châtelet); *Five Gold Rings* (Almeida); *Beauty and the Beast, Bartholomew Fair* (Royal Shakespeare Company); *Cider House Rules* (Atlantic); *Power Plays* (Manhattan Theatre Club); *A Day in the Death of Joe Egg* (Broadway).

Dance includes: *The Rite of Spring, Petrushka, Rian* (Sadler's Wells); *Aeternum* (Royal Ballet).

Opera includes: *The Last Hotel, Andre Chenier, Adriana Lecouvreur* (Royal Opera House); *Un Ballo in Maschera* (Metropolitan Opera); *Norma, Power Her Face, Julius Caesar, Peter Grimes* (ENO).

Carolyn Downing

Sound

Carolyn is an award-winning sound designer working across a variety of fields.

Previous Young Vic includes: *Blackta, After Miss Julie.*

Other theatre includes: *As You Like It, Our Country's Good, The Motherf***er with the Hat, Dara* (National Theatre); *Chimerica (*Almeida & SFP, winner of the Olivier Award for Best Sound Design 2014); *Carmen Disruption* (Almeida); *Les Liaisons Dangereuses, Teddy Ferrara, Fathers and Sons* (Donmar Warehouse); *The Believers, Beautiful Burnout, Love Song* (Frantic Assembly); *Hope, The Pass, The Low Road, Choir Boy* (Royal Court); *The House That Will Not Stand, Handbagged* (Tricycle/West End); *Thérèse Raquin* (Theatre Royal Bath); *Twelfth Night* (Crucible); *Much Ado About Nothing, To Kill a Mockingbird* (Royal Exchange).

Opera includes: *Benjamin, Dernière Nuit* (Lyon Opera); *How the Whale Became* (ROH).

Exhibitions include: *So You Say You Want a Revolution? Records and Rebels 1965–1970* (V&A, from Autumn 2016); *Exhibitionism: The Rolling Stones* (Saatchi); *Collider* (Science Museum); *Louis Vuitton: Series 3* (London).

Carolyn has also created sound design elements for Louis Vuitton shows at the Louis Vuitton Foundation, Paris.

Joseph Alford

Movement

Joseph is Co-Artistic Director of theatre O. He studied at the École Internationale de Théâtre and has a BA (Hons) in Drama and English from the University of East Anglia. He is a theatre maker, director and movement director.

Previous Young Vic includes: *The Secret Agent* (as director; theatre O/Young Vic); *The Cherry Orchard, Happy Days, Blackta* (as movement director); *The Way Back Home* (as associate director and movement director; Young Vic/ENO), *The Cat in the Hat* (as movement director; Young Vic/National Theatre), *How Much Is Your Iron?* (as performer).

Other directing includes: *The Man Jesus* (Lyric Belfast); *Delirium* (Barbican/Abbey Theatre, Dublin); *The Bridge* (Laban Centre/tour); *Astronaut, The Argument; Three Dark Tales* (Barbican/international tour).

Movement directing work includes: *Cleansed, A Woman Killed with Kindness, Beauty and the Beast* (National); *Alcina* (Festival d'Aix en Provence); *Lucia de Lammermoor, How the Whale Became, Clemency* (ROH); *Play House* (Orange Tree); *The Trial of Ubu* (Hampstead); *Idomeneo* (ENO).

Emma Woodvine

Voice

Previous Young Vic includes: *Macbeth, Happy Days, The Scottsboro Boys, American Lulu, A Season in the Congo, The Changeling, A Doll's House, After Miss Julie, Beloved, I Am Yusuf, This Is My Brother.*

Other theatre includes: *The Glass Menagerie* (Nuffield Theatre); *Richard II, Henry V, Henry IV Part 1, Henry IV Part 2, The Two Gentlemen of Verona, The Witch of Edmonton, The Jew of Malta, Love's Sacrifice* (RSC); *Hang, Routes* (Royal Court); *Hitchcock Blonde* (Hull Truck); *Kiss Me Kate, Carousel* (Opera North/Barbican); *Pitchfork Disney* (Arcola); *The Winter's Tale, 'Tis Pity She's* a Whore, Macbeth (Cheek by Jowl); Noises Off (Old Vic); Othello (Sheffield Crucible); Ghost the Musical (Piccadilly); The School for Scandal (Barbican); Breakfast at Tiffany's (Theatre Royal Haymarket); 11 and 12 (Peter Brook at the Barbican); The Fastest Clock in the Universe (Hampstead); As You Like It (Watford Palace).

Television includes: Christopher and His Kind.

Julia Horan CDG
Casting

Julia is an Associate Artist at the Young Vic.

Previous Young Vic includes: The Trial, Ah, Wilderness!, Happy Days, Man: Three plays by Tennessee Williams, A View from the Bridge (also Wyndham's/New York), Public Enemy, The Shawl, Blackta, A Doll's House (also Duke of York's/BAM), After Miss Julie, The Government Inspector, The Events (also ATC), Wild Swans (also ART), Joe Turner's Come and Gone, Glass Menagerie, Annie Get Your Gun.

Other theatre includes: Harry Potter and the Cursed Child (Palace); Hamlet (Barbican); Uncle Vanya, Medea, Oresteia (also Trafalgar Studios), Game, Mr Burns, Chimerica (also Harold Pinter), Before the Party, King Lear, Children's Children, The Homecoming (Almeida); Hope, Teh Internet Is Serious Business, Wolf from the Door, The Nether (also Duke of York's), Adler and Gibb, Birdland, Khandan, The Mistress Contract, The Pass, Wastwater, Tribes, Clybourne Park (also Wyndham's); Spur of the Moment, Sucker Punch (Royal Court); The Lighthouse Keeper (BCMG); Red Velvet (Tricycle/St Ann's Warehouse/Garrick).

Film includes: The Kaiser's Last Kiss; Departure.

Michal Keyamo
Assistant Director

Since graduating as a Bachelor of Law in 2013, Michal has focused on work as a director and performer.

Previous Young Vic includes: Macbeth (as trainee assistant director), 'Introduction to Directing' course (led by Ben Kidd), Red Forest (as cast).

Theatre as director includes: Intermission Theatre's 10-10-10 Festival; New Heritage Theatre's Scratch Night; several research and development projects working as director and facilitator.

Theatre as actor includes: King Lear (Globe); Handa's Surprise (Little Angel Theatre/tour).

JERWOOD
CHARITABLE FOUNDATION

Young Vic It's a big world in here

Our shows

We present the widest variety of classics, new plays, forgotten works and music theatre. We tour and co-produce extensively within the UK and internationally.

Our artists

Our shows are created by some of the world's great theatre people alongside the most adventurous of the younger generation. This fusion makes the Young Vic one of the most exciting theatres in the world.

Our audience

. . . is famously the youngest and most diverse in London. We encourage those who don't think theatre is 'for them' to make it part of their lives. We give 10 per cent of our tickets to schools and neighbours irrespective of box-office demand, and keep prices low.

Our partners near at hand

Each year we engage with 10,000 local people – individuals and groups of all kinds including schools and colleges – by exploring theatre on and off stage. From time to time we invite our neighbours to appear on our stage alongside professionals.

Our partners further away

By co-producing with leading theatre, opera and dance companies from London and around the world we create shows neither partner could achieve alone.

The Cut Bar and Restaurant

Our bar and restaurant is a relaxing place to meet and eat. An inspired mix of classic and original play-themed dishes made from fresh, free-range and organic ingredients creates an exciting menu.

www.thecutbar.com

The Young Vic is a company limited by guarantee, registered in England No. 1188209

VAT registration No. 236 673 348

The Young Vic (registered charity No 268876) received public funding from

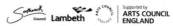

markit

Lead sponsor of the Young Vic's funded ticket scheme

Get more from the Young Vic online

Sign up to receive email updates at youngvic.org/register

 youngvictheatre

 @youngvictheatre

 youngviclondon

 youngviclondon.wordpress.com

 @youngvictheatre

THE YOUNG VIC COMPANY

GET INVOLVED WITH THE YOUNG VIC

'The best theatre in London'   Telegraph

'One of our favourite theatres, as bustling and unorthodox as ever'   Sunday Times

'The work has been sensational. Some of the best international directors, great performers with the chance to play their dream roles'   Independent

'London's glorious temple of leftfield theatre'   Time Out

To produce our sell-out, award-winning shows and provide thousands of free activities through our Taking Part programme requires major investment. Find out how you can make a difference and get involved.

As an individual . . . become a Friend, donate to a special project, attend our unique gala events or remember the Young Vic in your will.

As a company . . . take advantage of our flexible memberships, exciting sponsorship opportunities, corporate workshops, CSR engagement and venue hire.

As a trust or foundation . . . support our innovative and forward-thinking programmes on stage and off.

Are you interested in events . . . hire a space in our award-winning building and we will work with you to create a memorable workshop, conference or party.

For more information visit:
youngvic.org/support us
020 7922 2810
Charity Registration No. 268876.

SUPPORTING THE YOUNG VIC

The Young Vic relies on the generous support of many individuals, trusts, foundations, and companies to produce our work, on and off stage. For their recent support we thank

Public Funders

Arts Council England
British Council
Creative & Cultural Skills
Lambeth Borough Council
Southwark Council

Corporate Partners

Barclays
Berkeley Group
Bloomberg
Edelman
Markit
Wahaca

Corporate Members

aka
Bloomberg
Clifford Chance
Edelman
Ingenious Media Plc
Memery Crystal
Mishcon de Reya
Royal Bank of Scotland
& NatWest
Wisdom Council

Partners and Upper Circle

Lionel Barber
The Bickertons
Tony & Gisela Bloom
Simon & Sally Borrows
Sandra Cavlov
Caroline & Ian Cormack
Manfred & Lydia Gorvy
Patrick Handley
Jack & Linda Keenan
Patrick McKenna
Simon & Midge Palley
Karl-Johan Persson
Barbara Reeves
Jon & Nora Lee Sedmak
Dasha Shenkman
Justin Shinebourne
Rita & Paul Skinner
Bruno Wang
Anda & Bill Winters

Soul Mates

David & Corinne Abbott
Jane Attias
Chris & Frances Bates
Ginny & Humphrey Battcock
Anthony & Karen Beare
Joanne Beckett
Royce & Rotha Bell
Sarah Billinghurst Solomon
Lisa & Adrian Binks
Eva Boenders & Scott Stevens

Beatrice Bondy
Katie Bradford
CJ & LM Braithwaite
Simon Brych-Nourry
Clive & Helena Butler
Kay Ellen Consolver
Lucy & Spencer de Grey
Annabel Duncan-Smith
Sean Egan
Jennifer & Jeff Eldredge
Don Ellwood & Sandra
Johnigan
Lysbeth Fox
Paul Gambaccini
Sarah Gay Fletcher
Jill & Jack Gerber
Beth & Gary Glynn
Rory Godson
Annika Goodwille
Sarah Hall
Katherine Hallgarten
Richard Hardman & Family
Frances Hellman
Nick Hern
Madeleine Hodgkin
Nik Holttum & Helen Brannigan
Jane Horrocks
Linden Ife
Maxine Isaacs
Clive Jones
Tom Keatinge
John Kinder & Gerry Downey
Mr & Mrs Herbert Kretzmer
Carol Lake
Martha Lane Fox
Jude Law
Victoira Leggett
Chris & Jane Lucas
Tony Mackintosh
James & Sue Macmillan
Jill & Justin Manson
Lady Medina Marks
Michael McCabe
Karen McHugh
Sir Ian McKellen
Barbara Minto
Miles Morland
Georgia Oetker
Rob & Lesley O'Rahilly
Barbara Reeves
Anthony & Sally Salz
Catherine Schreiber
Carol Sellars
Dr Bhagat Sharma
Nicola Stanhope
Sir Patrick Stewart
Jan & Michael Topham
Totally Theatre Productions
The Ulrich Family
Donna & Richard Vinter
Jimmy & Carol Walker

Rob & Gillian Wallace
Edgar & Judith Wallner

Trust Supporters

Amberstone Trust
Andor Charitable Trust
Austin & Hope Pilkington
Trust
Backstage Trust
Boris Karloff Charitable
Foundation
The City Bridge Trust
The Cleopatra Trust
Clifford Chance Foundation
Clore Duffield Foundation
Cockayne — Grants for the Arts
John S Cohen Foundation
The Dr Mortimer and Theresa
Sackler Foundation
D'Oyly Carte Charitable Trust
Embassy of the Kingdom
of the Netherlands
Equitable Charitable Trust
The Eranda Foundation
Ernest Cook Trust
The Foyle Foundation
Garfield Weston Foundation
Garrick Charitable Trust
Genesis Foundation
Golden Bottle Trust
Golsoncott Foundation
The Harold Hyam Wingate
Foundation
Jerwood Charitable Foundation
John Thaw Foundation
J Paul Getty Jnr Charitable
Trust
The Kidron and Hall Family
The Leche Trust
The Limbourne Trust
The London Community
Foundation
The Mackintosh Foundation
The Martin Bowley Charitable
Trust
The Sir Noël Coward
Foundation
The Portrack Charitable Trust
The Rayne Trust
The Red Hill Trust
Richard Radcliffe Charitable
Trust
The Richenthal Foundation
Royal Victoria Hall
Foundation
The Sackler Trust
Unity Theatre Trust
The Wolfson Foundation
*and all other donors who wish
to remain anonymous.*

markit®

Proud to be the lead sponsor of the Funded Ticket Programme

Through Markit's support, the Young Vic offers nearly 10,000 free tickets to young people and many that would not otherwise be able to enjoy the theatre.

markit.com

Blue/Orange

For my Dad,
the late, great Brian Penhall (1933–1998)

Blue/Orange was first performed in the Cottesloe auditorium of the National Theatre, London, on 7 April 2000. The cast was as follows:

Christopher	Chiwetel Ejiofor
Bruce	Andrew Lincoln
Robert	Bill Nighy

Directed by Roger Michell
Designed by William Dudley

Michael Codron and Lee Dean transferred the National Theatre production to the Duchess Theatre on 30 April 2001.

Characters

Christopher, *twenty-four*
Bruce, *twenties*
Robert, *fifties*

Setting

The action takes place over twenty-four hours in a modern
NHS psychiatric hospital in London.

Act One

A consultation room. A transparent water cooler. A round table with a large glass bowl containing three oranges.

Bruce *and* **Christopher** *stand facing each other.*

Christopher   Mister Bruce –

Bruce   Christopher –

Christopher   Mister Bruce –

Bruce   How are you doing?

Christopher   Brucey Brucey Brucey. How you doing?

Bruce   A pleasure as always.

Christopher   A pleasure. Yeah, a pleasure. The pleasure's all mine, man.

Bruce   Take a seat.

Christopher   The pleasure today is mine. D'you know what I mean?

Bruce   Plant your arse.

Christopher   It's mine! It's my day. Innit. My big day. What can I say . . . ?

Bruce   Yes, well, yes – sit down now.

Christopher   Gimme some skin.

Bruce   Why not.

Bruce *shakes* **Christopher**'s *hand.* **Christopher** *makes it an elaborate one. They punch fists.*

Christopher   I'm a free man. D'you know what I mean?

Bruce   Well . . . aha ha . . . OK.

Christopher   I'm a happy man. Bursting with joy.

Bruce   Chris?

Christopher   Oh – hey – oh . . . OK. I'll be good. You're right. I should sit.

Christopher *sits with exaggerated calm.*

Bruce   Relax.

Christopher   I should relax and calm myself.

Bruce   Take a few breaths. Would you like some water?

Christopher (*fidgeting*)   Uh?

Bruce   Would you like a cup of water?

Christopher   Coke.

Bruce   No, you can't have –

Christopher   Ice-cold Coke. The Real Thing.

Bruce   No, you know you can't have Coke –

Christopher   Yeah I can because –

Bruce   What did I tell you about Coke?

Christopher   I'm going home tomorrow.

Bruce   What's wrong with drinking Coke?

Christopher   But I'm going home.

Bruce   Chris? Come on you know this, it's important. What's wrong with Coke?

Pause.

Christopher   It rots your teeth.

Bruce   No – well, yes – and . . . ? What else does it do to you?

Christopher   Makes my head explode.

Bruce   Well – no – no – what does it do to you really?

Christopher   Makes my head explode – oh man – I know – I get you.

Bruce   It's not good for you, is it?

Christopher   No. It's bad.

Bruce   What's the first thing we learnt when you came in here?

Christopher   No coffee no Coke.

Bruce   No coffee no Coke, that's right. Doesn't do us any good at all.

Christopher   Mm.

Bruce   Gets us overexcited.

Christopher   Yeah yeah yeah yeah, makes me jumpy.

Bruce   That's right so – what shall we have instead?

Christopher   I dunno.

Bruce   What would you like?

Christopher   What I'd really like is a Snakebite. D'you know what I mean?

Bruce   A Snakebite. Right, well –

Christopher   Cider and Red Stripe or, you know, or a rum and black or or or . . .

Bruce   Chris, Christopher . . . what's the rule on alcohol now?

Christopher   But –

Bruce   What's the rule on alcohol in here?

Christopher   Alcohol.

Pause.

Oh yeah. Alcohol. Heh heh. D'you know what I mean?

Bruce   What does alcohol do?

Christopher   It makes your blood thin.

Bruce   No . . . well, possibly, but –

Christopher   Makes you see things.

Bruce   Well . . . yes, but –

Christopher   See into the future maybe.

Bruce   Well . . . s . . . sometimes maybe but what does it mostly do?

Christopher   It fucks you up.

Bruce   It fucks you up. Precisely. How about a glass of water. Eh? Some nice cool water? From the, from the thing?

Christopher   Water from the thing. That's cool.

Bruce   Nice cool water, yes. Let me – just hold on . . .

Bruce *gets up and* **Christopher** *suddenly gets up too.*

Bruce   No no – you're all right, I'm just –

Christopher   No, you're all right –

Bruce (*sitting*)   Help yourself –

Christopher (*sitting*)   No no, I'll –

Bruce   I'll – look – this is silly.

Bruce *gestures.*

Christopher   Are you sure?

Bruce   Be my guest.

Christopher *gets up and goes to the water cooler, takes two cups, pours.*

Bruce   Sorted.

Christopher (*drinking shakily*)   Sorted for Es and whiz.

Bruce   . . . Indeed.

Christopher   Sorted, innit. Sorted for Es and whiz.

Bruce   Absolutely.

Christopher (*sitting*)   D'you know what I mean? Heh heh. You must know what I mean? Eh? Eh? *Doctor*.

He puts a cup of water in front of **Bruce** *and sips his own.*

Christopher   D'you know what I mean?

Bruce   Huh. Of course . . .

Christopher   D'you know what I mean?

Bruce   Well . . .

Pause.

No. I don't.

Christopher   Yeah you do.

Bruce *sips his water.*

Christopher   Where's the *drugs*, man?

Bruce   . . . Oh the *drugs*. Of course . . .

Christopher   It's all that, innit. 'Where's the drugs, man? Oh man, these patients giving me massive big headache, man, massive big headache, what have I got in my doctor's bag, gimme some smack, where's some smack? Where's the Tamazie Party? This bad nigga patient I got. This *bad nigga dude* I know. My God! I Can't Take The Pressure!' Innit? Innit. Go home to the old lady – 'Aw I can't take the pressure. Oh no. I can't calm down. Oh no – yes – no – I can't shag until you gimme the smack, darling!' D'you know what I mean? Ha ha ha ha ha. Oh no. Ha ha. It's all that. You with me?

Pause.

Bruce   Well . . .

Christopher   Yeah yeah . . . go on! Typical white doctor. This is how *white* doctors speak: 'Drugs? What drugs? No drugs for *you*, nigga. Cos you'll only enjoy them! These are *my* drugs . . .'

Bruce   It's not quite like that.

Christopher   Deny. It's all you doctors do! Deny, man.

Bruce   Well, I don't think so really . . .

Christopher (*sipping water shakily*)   Bullshit. Bullshit. Why else would you do it? Why else are you here?

Bruce   Well, Christopher, why do you think you're here?

Christopher   Eh?

Bruce   Why are you here? Why do you think you're here?

Christopher   Why am I here?

Bruce   Yes.

Pause.

Christopher   I dunno.

Bruce   And you've been here a while now.

Christopher   Yeah – yes I have . . . that's true.

Bruce   Why do you think that is? If you'd just wanted drugs you wouldn't really be here, would you? You'd be out there. Scoring off somebody and . . . going home. Wouldn't you?

Pause.

I know I would! Eh? Ha ha. Have a smoke. Watch the football.

Pause.

N'ha ha.

Pause.

No. Obviously. I'm not a drug user – OK? You know. But joking aside – it doesn't make sense that anybody would be in here just for drugs as opposed to say, you know, out there *enjoying*, enjoying their drugs. Having some fun. D'you see what I mean?

Pause.

I mean, they are supposed to be recreational.

Pause.

So my point is – and this is one of the things I want to talk to you about today – you're here to get better, aren't you? Because you've been very poorly. Haven't you?

Long pause.

Christopher   I dunno.

Bruce   Ah.

Christopher   What's up? I'm going home. You should be happy.

Bruce   Well, I'm not as happy as you.

Christopher   I been saying all along, there's nothing wrong with me and now you agree with me and, I just, I just, I just . . . I'm going home.

Pause.

I don't know why I'm here.

Pause.

It's mad, innit. It's bonkers. Mad shit. First thing I said when I arrived. When I first come in here. I had a look, I saw all the all the, you know, the others, the other geezers and I thought . . . Fuck This. My God! These people are insane! Ha ha ha ha ha . . . Get Me Outta Here –

Bruce   Ha ha yes –

Christopher   It's a *nut*house, man.

Bruce   I grant you – indeed – there are a fair proportion –

Christopher   A *fair proportion*? You're kidding me.

Bruce   Of quite, quite –

Christopher   They are NUTS!

Bruce   . . . crazy people here . . . yes –

Christopher   Crazies, man! Radio Rental.

Bruce   People with – well – we don't actually use the term 'crazy' . . .

Christopher   You just said it.

Bruce   I know I just said it but – I shouldn't have – I was – humouring – I was, you know – it's a no-no.

Christopher   But you just said it.

Bruce   I know, but – you see my point?

Christopher   You said it first.

Bruce   OK, look . . . there are things we . . . there are terms we use which people used to use all the time, terms which used to be inoffensive but things are a bit different now. Certain words.

Christopher   Certain words, what words?

Bruce   Just . . . terms which aren't even that offensive but –

Christopher   Same as I say, what's offensive about it?

Bruce   Well –

Christopher   It's true!

Bruce   It's not true . . . it's – OK – it's not even that – it's just inaccurate. Some terms are just inaccurate. 'Crazy' is one of them. It's just . . . unhelpful. Woolly.

Christopher   'Woolly'. Oh. OK. I'm sorry.

Bruce   For example, people used to say 'schizophrenic' all the time. 'Such-and-such is schizophrenic.' Because it's two things at once. OK. Used to denote a divided agenda, a dual identity, the analogy of a split personality. Except we know now that schizophrenia doesn't mean that at all. Split personality? Meaningless. OK? So it's an unhelpful term. It's inaccurate. What we call a 'misnomer'. And this is a sensitive subject. We must think carefully, be *specific*. Because it's too . . . you know . . . it's too serious.

Pause.

You were diagnosed with 'Borderline Personality Disorder'. What does that mean?

Pause.

Borderline personality disorder. OK? Key word – *borderline*. Because, clinically speaking, you're on the *border* between neurotic and psychotic.

Christopher   Just . . . on the border.

Bruce   Yes. And that's a very useful term, isn't it? Because if people get the word wrong – if people just get the meaning of the word wrong, how can they get the person right? How can there be any . . . any awareness? People don't know anything about it. They have stupid ideas. You lose out. So we try to 'demystify'. We try to explain.

Pause.

Which is what I wanted to talk to you about today. Your diagnosis. This term, this label, and what it means, because the thing is, I'm beginning to think, now . . . it's . . . well, it's a little inaccurate –

Christopher   YOU'VE MADE YOUR POINT I SAID I'M SORRY WHAT DO YOU WANT – BLOOD?

Bruce   But I'm just saying . . . in the light of recent developments –

Christopher   Developments? What developments. What you on about, man?

Robert, *carrying a cup of coffee also in a plastic cup, appears at the door and just stands there waiting.*

Robert   You wanted to see me.

Bruce   Doctor Smith. Yes, come in. Hi.

Robert   How's tricks?

Bruce   I'm fine. How are you?

Robert   I don't believe I've thanked you for that stupendous spread.

Bruce   Sorry?

Robert   That sumptuous meal on Saturday. After the rugby. The food.

Bruce   Oh. Thanks.

Robert   Hang on to that woman, Bruce.

Bruce   Sure.

Robert   You'll live to a hundred and three.

Bruce   The thing is –

Robert   The only woman I know with the audacity to pull off a fondue. I thought, 'Any minute now she'll be climbing into her caftan.'

Bruce   It was Welsh rarebit.

Robert   Welsh rarebit? The very thing.

Bruce   I know it's not what you're used to –

Robert   On the contrary. It was just the ticket. Miserable and wet. Vanquished by the Frog and foot-sore.

Bruce   Well, it soaked up the booze.

Robert   I couldn't believe that score. Not from the Frogs. Still, at least it wasn't Australia –

Bruce   Doctor Smith –

Robert   Or New Zealand or any of the other hairy colonial outposts.

Bruce   Doctor –

Robert   Welsh rarebit, eh? Took me back to my student days. Tie that woman to the nearest bed and inseminate her at once.

Bruce   Doctor –

Robert   *Breed*. Lots of little Bruces. Have you thought any more about that loft conversion? All the rage when I was a student. Quite the thing for somebody in your circumstances.

Robert *winks at* **Christopher** *conspiratorially and* **Christopher** *just stares back blankly.*

Bruce   Doc –

Robert   That'll set you back a few quid. Still, when you become a consultant . . .

Bruce   D –

Robert   That's where the big bucks are.

Bruce   The thing is –

Robert (*to* **Christopher**)   Hello.

Bruce   You remember Christopher? Chris, do you remember Doctor Smith? Senior Consultant.

Christopher   Warning warning warning! Alien life form approaching, Will Robinson.

Robert   Mm, ha ha ha –

Bruce   Mm, yes –

Robert   Very witty –

Bruce   OK . . . look –

Christopher   Warning warning warning . . . d'you know what I mean?

Bruce   Let's not get too distracted.

Robert   I'm distracting you of course.

Bruce   No no, you –

Robert   I –

Bruce   I want you to –

Robert   Well, of course, you asked me to –

Christopher   D'you know what I mean?

Bruce   I've asked Doctor Smith to sit in today.

Robert   Yes that's right. Just got myself a nice cup of coffee and I'll just lurk in the corner . . .

Christopher (*simultaneously with 'corner'*)   Coffee . . . !

Robert   You won't know I'm here.

Christopher   He's got coffee.

Bruce   There's plenty of water in the –

Christopher   Oh wow!

Bruce   That's not for you.

Christopher (*reaching over and gesturing for coffee*)   Oh come on, man. Coffee!

Bruce   Chris . . . Chris . . . (*To* **Robert**.) Excuse me.

Christopher   I want a cup of coffee.

Bruce   Christopher, hey listen, that's not yours.

Christopher   I'll split it with you.

Bruce   Is that yours or isn't it?

Christopher   Come on, man.

Bruce   Chris . . . Chris, come on! What's the rule on coffee?

Christopher *sits and kisses his teeth.*

Bruce   No Coke no coffee. I'm sorry. You know why.

Christopher   Why?

Bruce   You know why.

Christopher   Yeah, but I get out tomorrow. I'm getting out.

Robert   I think your man has a point.

Bruce *looks at* **Robert**.

Robert *takes out a packet of cigarettes and lights one.*

Robert   Sorry. I'm distracting you.

Robert *gets up to leave but* **Bruce** *gestures for him to sit.*

Bruce   Please, you aren't. Really.

Christopher   You got cigarettes! Gimme a cigarette, Doc, just one, I'm gagging for a puff, d'you know what I mean?

Bruce *nods.*

Robert *sits again and offers the pack to* **Christopher** *who takes a cigarette, then another, then another two, putting one behind his ear, two in his top pocket and one in his mouth.*

Robert *lights the cigarette for him and* **Christopher** *exhales a plume of smoke.*

Robert   Better?

Christopher   It's my nerves. I'm getting out tomorrow. You can't tell me what to do when I get out – when I'm out there – which is in (*checks his watch*) exactly twenty-four hours. I'm not under your . . . it's none of your business then, man. I'm twenty-four hours away from freedom. Out of this hole. D'you know what I mean?

Pause.

Forty-eight hours tops.

Robert   Give him some coffee, he's going home. I haven't touched mine.

Robert *offers the coffee,* **Christopher** *reaches for it but* **Bruce** *is there first and takes the cup, drains it in one and throws it expertly into a waste-paper bin in the corner.*

Christopher   Hey, man –

Bruce   Coffee's got caffeine in it.

Robert   Or a nice cup of tea?

Bruce   So has tea. The water's over there.

Christopher   What did you do that for?

Robert   If this isn't a good time . . . ?

Bruce   No, it's perfect timing. I wanted you to see this.

Robert   See what?

Christopher   I'm already *packed*.

Bruce   You're packed?

Robert   I'll just –

Christopher   Yeah, man. What, you think I'm not in a hurry? (*To* **Robert**.) I could use a coffee to give me a bump. Just to get me on my way, d'you know what I mean?

Bruce   Who said you could pack?

Robert (*half standing, hovering*)   Look, I can just –

Christopher   No one, man, I just did it. I just (no, you stay there), I put my pyjamas in a bag and my toothbrush in on top. (Don't move.) Took a whole five minutes. Shoot me. What, you think I 'pinched the towels' and some stationery?

Bruce   The thing is . . .

Christopher   Cos I'm I'm I'm . . . I'm what?

Robert   I can come back –

Christopher   Because I'm . . . ? (No you're all right.) Cos I'm . . . ?

Bruce   No –

Christopher   I'm –

Bruce   No –

Christopher   No what? You don't even know what I was gonna say. What was I gonna say?

Robert   Or I can stay?

Bruce   No, no I wasn't –

Christopher   Because I'm a Brother?

Pause.

Bruce (*to* **Robert**)   Paranoia. Nihilism. Persecution. Delusion –

Christopher   Cos I'm an 'uppity nigga'.

Bruce   No. You always say that and I always tell you the same thing. No.

Robert   I'll come back, shall I?

Bruce   Doctor Smith –

Christopher   WOULD YOU JUST MAKE UP YOUR MIND BEFORE I GO STARK STARING BANANAS? Bouncing about like Zebedee.

Bruce   Christopher –

Christopher   Don't Christopher me, man . . . (One sip of coffee he thinks he's Batman.)

Bruce   You know that's not the way you talk to the consultants.

Christopher   He's giving me the fear.

Bruce   Calm down. Now you are acting like a –

Christopher   A what? A what. Go on, say it. An 'uppity nigga'.

Christopher *kisses his teeth and starts eyeballing* **Robert**.

Bruce   Well . . . OK, yes, frankly you are and that's not what we do, is it? Eh? And when you get out of here, if you start staring at people like that, what are they going to think?

Christopher   What?

Bruce   What are people going to think? When you get out? When you're ready . . . ?

Christopher   I don't fucking know.

Bruce   Well, what do you think they're gonna think?

Christopher   I don't know.

Bruce   They'll think you're a, a, an 'uppity nigga', that's what they'll think. Kissing your teeth. It's not you. It's silly. It's crazy. You're not a, a, a, some type of '*Yardie*' –

Christopher   Now you're telling me who I am?

Bruce   No, I'm –

Christopher   You're telling me who I am?

Bruce   I'm telling you . . . to be You.

Christopher   That's rum, that is. That's rich. Now I've got an identity crisis. You're a cheeky fucking monkey, you are, aren't you?

Pause.

Robert   Mm. 'Uppity' isn't strictly speaking a term we –

Bruce (*to* **Robert**)   Learned Unresponsiveness? Disorganised Behaviour? Decline in Social Skills? Do you get me?

Robert   So?

Bruce   Eh?

Robert   Look around you. *Who isn't* unresponsive, and disorganised with declining social skills? Eh? Heh heh. It's *normal*.

Pause.

Uh-huh huh huh.

Bruce   Could we have a quiet word?

Christopher *stands abruptly and slams his fist on the desk.*

Christopher   Hey! You! I'm talking to you. When I get out of this place, people won't think *anything* because I'll be gone, boy. I'm going far away where I can get some peace and quiet, no people, no cars, pollution, planes flying overhead like fruit flies, no cities, no fucking TVs, no construction work, no roadworks, no drills, no neighbours squatting on my head, under the floor, through the walls, rowing all day and night. Nothing. No people at all, man, and nobody looking at me funny like they never seen a Brother before except on fucking *Sesame Street*! I'm going far away. (What's he looking at?) Look at you – nervous as a tomcat with big balls.
D'you think I'm gonna eat you?
I might do just to see the look on your face.

Bruce   Nobody's looking at you funny, Chris.

Christopher   He is.

Robert   Well, are you surprised?

Christopher   What?

Robert   Are you surprised? Look at yourself. Now just . . . sit down and . . . relax, would you? Of course people stare at you when you act like this. You know that, you know what it's like.

Christopher *looks from one to another, kisses his teeth.*

Pause.

Bruce (*to* **Robert**)   Overburdened Nervous System. Can't look me in the eye. Thinks we're staring at him.

Robert   We are.

Pause.

Christopher   I'm gone, oh yes. Believe. A place with a desert. And beaches. Palm trees. Somewhere hot. D'you know what I mean?

Bruce   Chris . . . ? Would you mind waiting in the other room for two minutes?

Christopher   What did I say?

Bruce   Nothing at all, we just need to –

Robert   Consult.

Bruce   That's right.

Robert   That's why the badge says 'Consultant'. (I'm not wearing it.)

Bruce   Please. I'd really appreciate it. Just go through that door.

Christopher (*sighs*)   OK. But I hope you know what you're doing, yeah?

Bruce   How do you mean?

Christopher   I hope you're not gonna let him talk you into anything.

Robert   Good God no. No no no no no.

Christopher   Hope you're not gonna go changing your mind on me. Cos my twenty-eight . . .

Bruce   Chris –

Christopher   My twenty-eight days –

Bruce   I know –

Christopher   My twenty-eight days is up. It's up, man. You've had your fun. I'm gone. Believe.

Bruce   Uh-huh, OK . . . thank you.

Christopher *stands, lingers, stares at them both, then goes through a door.*

Silence.

Bruce   Do you think he knows?

Robert   What's there to know? He's a Section 2. His twenty-eight days are up. He's responded to treatment and now he's going home.

Pause.

Am I right?

Bruce   But –

Robert   But what?

Bruce   Well . . . I mean, you know what I'm going to ask you, don't you?

Pause.

Robert   What?

Bruce   I want a Section 3.

Robert   Take a deep breath, and forget you even thought of it.

Bruce   But –

Robert   Let him out. You're doing the right thing.

Bruce   But I'm not.

Robert   Yes, this is right. You are doing what is fair and right and *just* and textbook medically beneficial.

Pause.

And apart from anything else we don't have the beds.

Bruce   I'm really quite concerned –

Robert   Those beds are Prioritised for Emergency Admissions and Level Ones. Otherwise we'll wind up with a hospital full of long-term chronic mental patients hurtling about on *trolleys* – it'll be like the *Wacky Races*.

Bruce   Look –

Robert   There'd be scandal. They'd have my arse out of here faster than his and you'd be next. That's right. I'll never make Professor. You'll never make your Specialist Registrar Training. And how long did you study for that? Six years? What were we saying on Saturday?

Bruce   When?

Robert   After the rugby. What did we talk about?

Bruce   I dunno, what?

Robert   Well, your Specialist Registrar Training. And I said, for the coming year I am prepared to supervise you, I'll be your 'Mentor', I'll teach you 'all I know' . . . but you have to play the game.

Bruce   'Play the game'?

Robert   That's right. I'll push your barrow. I'll feed the scrum but you're going to have to kick the ball into touch once in a while.

Bruce   But –

Robert   Take my advice, if you keep your nose clean and you enjoy psychiatry you'll almost certainly become a consultant. Nevertheless, you don't want to be a consultant for ever. Sooner or later you'll want to become a Senior. You too may one day seek a professorship.

Bruce   If I . . . ?

Robert   But you can't afford to be indecisive about this.

Bruce   But I *am* indecisive.

Robert   You can't afford not to follow my advice is what I mean.

Bruce   Oh, that kind of indecisive.

Robert   They'll close the hospital down and build another Millennium Dome.

Bruce   Nobody's going to close the hospital because of one Section 3. Are they? D'you think . . . ?

Robert   Yes. Perhaps.

Bruce   Really?

Robert   Yes. Perhaps.

Pause.

Follow the Path of Least Resistance.

Bruce   But . . . I can't justify throwing him out on the basis of beds.

Robert   You're not 'throwing him out' . . . you're doing what we are here to do. What *they* are here for us to do – and what everybody *expects* us to do.

Pause.

Eh? You are giving this man his *freedom*.
You are releasing this man into the bosom of the community.
You are giving him back his life.
He's going back to his people.

Bruce   His 'people'? He doesn't have any *people*. He doesn't have a life.

Robert   That's a matter of conjecture.

Bruce   It's true. He's on the White City Estate. It's a predominantly Jamaican community, he didn't grow up there, he doesn't know anybody and he hates it.

Robert   Where did he grow up?

Bruce   All over the place. Peripatetic childhood.

Robert   What about family? He must have a mother.

Bruce   He doesn't seem to be in contact with her any more.

Robert   Are you proposing to section this man again on the basis that he – what – he's lonely?

Bruce   It'll do his head in.

Robert   It'll do his head in if you section him again.

Bruce   He isn't ready to go. You heard him. He's unstable.

Robert   Borderline personality disorder. On the border of neurotic and psychotic.

Bruce   He was highly animated, shouting, staring.

Robert   You'd shout and stare if you were on the border of neurotic and psychotic.

Bruce   The loosening of associations? The paranoia?

Robert   And you can add, reckless, impulsive, prone to extreme behaviour, problems handling personal life, handling money, maintaining a home, family, sex, relationships, alcohol, a fundamental inability to handle practically everything that makes us human – and hey, Some People Are Just *Like* That. Borderline. On the border. Occasionally visits but doesn't live there. See, technically he's not *that* mentally ill. We can't keep him here. It's Ugly but it's Right.

Pause.

Shoot me, those are the rules.

Bruce   'Shoot me'? 'Some people are just like that. Shoot me'? Are you joking?

Robert   Deadly serious. It's what makes it so hard for us. And one day, when you're a consultant like me, and you will be, if you don't fuck this up, when every young clinician is saying exactly the same thing as you, you'll tell them what I'm telling you now. Some People Are Just Like That. Get over it. We hold their hands for twenty-eight days, wait until things have calmed down, the mess has been mopped up and off they trot, back to whatever hell they've just blown in from, usually a little bit happier and maybe even a little bit wiser until the next time.

Pause.

Bruce   Christopher is a schizophrenic.

Pause.

Did you hear me?

Robert   No, he's BPD.

Bruce   If you Section 3 him I can keep him here until he's properly diagnosed.

Robert   No. Absolutely not.

Bruce   He's a Type I Schizophrenic with Positive Symptoms including Paranoid Tendencies. Probably Thought Disorder as well.

Robert   Not Paranoid Schizophrenia?

Bruce   Close but I'd be loath to go that far at this –

Robert   It's another month before we can diagnose Schizophrenia – Paranoid or Disorganised.

Bruce   So resection him.

Robert   Is he delusional?

Bruce   Sometimes.

Robert   Since when?

Bruce   Since he presented.

Robert   How delusional?

Bruce   Give me time and I'll show you.

Robert   You haven't got time. He's been here a month. He's been steadily improving – it's therefore a brief Psychotic Episode associated with BPD. Nothing more insidious.

Bruce   He's paranoid. You heard him.

Robert   How does BPD with Paranoia sound? Stick to the ICD 10 Classification.

Bruce   You love the ICD 10, don't you? All the different euphemisms for 'he's nuts' without actually having to admit he's nuts. It's like your Linus blanket.

Robert   OK. BPD and A Bit Nuts.

Bruce   No. Doctor. Please.

Robert   'Eccentric'.

Bruce   Look –

Robert   Was he squiffy?

Bruce   . . . 'Squiffy'?

Robert   'Squiffy'. Intoxicated. When he was sectioned.

Bruce   . . . Yes . . . I think . . .

Robert   BPD with Alcoholism. It's a movable feast.

Bruce   What? No it's not!

Robert   It's a matter of 'opinion'. And I'd be loath to resection the boy on the basis of a difference of opinion. It's semantics. And right now, Doctor, my semantics are better than yours so I win.

Bruce   I can't live with that diagnosis.

Robert   *You* don't have to.

Bruce   I can't live with the *prognosis*.

Robert   Well, you can't make a new diagnosis safely for at least another month.

Bruce   And I can't keep him another month unless I make a new diagnosis!

Pause.

Robert   But what's he done?

Bruce   He hasn't done anything yet.

Robert   Has he tried to harm himself?

Bruce   No.

Robert   Has he tried to harm anybody else?

Bruce   Of course not.

Robert   Well, you can't section him again until he does something. Is he a danger to himself or to the public is what I'm getting at.

Bruce   You want to wait until he becomes dangerous?

Robert   We have to be sure.

Bruce   But we can't be sure until it's too late.

Robert   And we can't do anything until he does something. It's a conundrum, I know.

Bruce   A 'conundrum'?

Robert   What's the risk factor? Come on. Write it down. Pretend you're running a business.

Bruce   'Pretend I'm . . . running a business'?

Robert   If we don't keep him in here – if we do not make this 'very costly outlay' . . .

Bruce   Well, it is risky.

Robert   How risky?

Bruce   *Very* risky.

Robert   What did he do before?

Bruce   Before when?

Robert   Before he was admitted. What happened?

Bruce   He was . . . he was in the market . . . doing . . . I dunno, something funny.

Robert   He was doing 'something funny' in the market. Which market?

Bruce   Does it matter?

Robert   I'm curious.

Bruce   Shepherd's Bush.

Robert   'Funny' strange or 'funny' ha ha?

Bruce   It's in the file. Read the file.

Robert   Why can't you just tell me?

Bruce   I'd rather not.

Robert   Why not?

Bruce   I'd just rather not.

Pause.

Robert   Why not?

Pause.

Why not, Doctor? What did he do?

Bruce   It's rather delicate.

Robert   Well, if you're going to be coy about it –

Bruce   I just don't think it's relevant.

Robert   We can't keep him in here unless he's dangerous. You know the rules.

Bruce   I think he's becoming depressed.

Robert   *I'm* becoming depressed now.

Pause.

Look.
Doctor. If you keep him here long enough he won't be able to go home because he won't know what home is any more. He won't know how it works any more – he won't know How To Do It. Get him out there now. Assign a community psychiatric nurse and treat him in the home – he's more comfortable, we're more comfortable, it's less of a drain on resources, the Authority is ecstatic.

Bruce   OK. In a perfect world, forgetting about 'resources', forgetting about 'budgetary constraints' – say we've got *unlimited beds* – what would you do?

Robert   In a perfect world I'd send him home with fucking bells on and spread a little happiness. Why the hell not? Now, you have a job to do. If you don't feel you can do that job, you go away and have a think for a while. You know, in the medical wilderness, in your new job proofreading for the fucking *Lancet*; writing Bolshevik columns for *Welsh Doctor Weekly*.

Pause.

Is he still in there? Where is he?

Bruce   He's in there.

Robert   In the . . . the . . .

Bruce   That little room.

Robert   What little room? The cleaners' room?

Bruce   No, the, you know. That little waiting room. That's where they go to wait. It's a new thing.

Pause.

Robert   You know, there is nothing wrong with your patient, Bruce. He may be a bit jumpy, he may be a bit brusque, a bit shouty, a bit OTT – but hey, maybe that's just what you do where he comes from.

Bruce   'Where he comes from'?

Robert   His 'community'.

Bruce   He comes from Shepherd's Bush. What exactly are you trying to say?

Robert   I'm not saying anything.

Bruce   'Where he comes from'? What are you saying?

Robert   I'm not saying anything.

Bruce   Go on. What are you saying?

Robert   Nothing.

Pause.

I'm only saying . . .

Pause.

Maybe . . . maybe, maybe it's just you. Maybe you just make him nervous. Eh?

Bruce   *What?*

Robert   Hear me out, it happens. This is the question we must ask ourselves. As a profession.

Bruce   'Is it me? Do I just make him nervous?'

Robert   Yes.

Bruce   He's a paranoid schizophrenic.

Robert   'Allegedly.'

Bruce   This is ridiculous.

Robert   We spend our lives asking whether or not this or that person is to be judged normal, a 'normal' person, a 'human', and we blithely assume that we know what 'normal' is. What 'human' is. Maybe he's more 'human' than us. Maybe *we're* the sick ones.

Bruce   He's 'more human than us'?

Robert   Yes.

Bruce   And we're the sick ones.

Robert   Maybe.

Pause.

Bruce   *Why?*

Silence.

Robert   OK, I'm being 'whimsical'. I'm being 'capricious'. But maybe, just maybe he's a *right* to be angry and paranoid and depressed and unstable. Maybe it's the only *suitable* response to the human condition.

Bruce What?

Robert The human species is the only species which is innately insane. 'Sanity is a conditioned response to environmental . . .

Bruce I don't believe you're saying this . . .

Robert . . . stimulae.' Maybe – just maybe it's true.

Bruce Maybe it's *utter horseshit*. (*Beat.*) I'm sorry. Doctor Smith. But. Which, which existential novelist said that? I mean, um, you'll be quoting R. D. Laing next.

Robert That was R. D. Laing.

Bruce R. D. Laing was a *madman*. They don't come any fruitier.

Robert I think there's something in it . . .

Bruce You'll be leaping into your tights and spouting Shakespeare next: Hamlet had a Borderline Personality Disorder with Morbidity, Recklessness, Impulsiveness and a propensity for dithering.

Robert He did!

Bruce Should you really be telling me this? Because, when I was at med school, you know, this is not the sort of thing I learnt.

Robert Well, with respect, Doctor, maybe it's time you grew up, eh? Loosen up, calm down, get your head out of your textbooks and learn a little about *humanity*. Humanity, Doctor. Being human. As the poet said, Allen Ginsberg, *Allen Ginsberg* said this, I'll never forget it . . . 'Human is not a noun, it's a *verb*.'

Pause.

Eh? Don't be so *old-fashioned*.

Silence.

Bruce Allen Ginsberg.

Robert   OK, bad example. But listen . . .
The government guidelines clearly state that the community
is the preferred and proper place and it's our duty to
subscribe to that. Otherwise it's no end of trouble.

Bruce   If I let him out he will have a breakdown and
succumb to all the most horrifying symptoms of
schizophrenia undiagnosed, unchecked, unsupervised and
unmedicated.

Robert   Doctor Flaherty –

Bruce   And we can't do anything about it –

Robert   Doctor Flaherty.

Bruce   Because of policy?

Robert   Calm down.

Bruce   I'm sorry. Um, you're right. I'm calm.

Robert   If you detain this man any longer he will become
institutionalised.
He won't get better he'll get worse.
You will make him ill.

Pause.

Bruce   Well, um, I don't believe I will.

Robert *goes to the door, opens it.*

Christopher *comes through the door.*

Robert   You can come back in now. We've finished our
little chat. Sit down, there's a good fellow. Can I get you
anything, a cup of water?

Robert *pours another cup for* **Christopher** *who drinks thirstily.*

Christopher *paces a moment.*

Bruce   Thirsty?

Christopher *nods and holds his cup out for a refill. He drinks it and
goes back to pacing.*

Bruce   That'll be the haloperidol. Are you still stiff?

Christopher   I'm jumping like a leaf. I been walking it off.

Bruce   Try not to.

Christopher   I like walking.

Bruce   I know. And that's how you get lost.

Christopher   I walked to the Hanger Lane Gyratory once.

Bruce   I know. I'm sure it was wonderful.

Robert   Bravo.

Bruce   No, not Bravo, you must try and control it.

Robert   Oh, let him walk if he wants to walk. Goodness gracious. You go ahead and walk to Hanger Lane. Enjoy. Now. When were you planning on leaving us?

Christopher (*pacing*)   Twenty-four hours.

Robert   Morning, evening?

Christopher   After I had my lunch.

Robert   And you have somewhere to go I take it.

Bruce   Council accommodation. White City.

Robert   Marvellous.

Christopher   Only I don't go there.

Robert   Oh.

Christopher   I don't like White City.

Robert   Why not?

Christopher   Cos of the Fuzz.

Robert   The 'Fuzz'.

Christopher   The Filth. The Pigs. The Cops. The 'Old Bill'.

Robert   The police?

Christopher   I get stopped a *lot* in White City.
That's why I was arrested in Shepherd's Bush. Cos they all
talk to each other on their walkie-talkies. They was waiting
for me. They came to get me in the market. Come all the way
from White City for me. Believe. I lost my shit.

Robert   I see, well –

Christopher   Cos they was after me, man.

Robert   And why do you think that is?

Christopher   What? *Why*?

Robert   Yes, why? Why were they 'after you'?

Christopher   Why do you *think*, man?

Robert   I'm asking you.

Christopher   Cos they're *fascists*. It's obvious.

Silence.

Robert   Where would you like to live?

Christopher   Where?

Robert   Would you prefer?

Christopher   Africa.

Robert   Africa.

Pause.

Christopher *sits and stares at* **Robert** *with intensity.*

Robert   Aha ha ha. Yes, very good. And why not?

Christopher   I already told you.

Robert   Yes, but I mean, for the time being.

Christopher   There is no time being. I'm going to Africa.
Central Africa. Where my dad come from.

Robert   Ah. Well . . . when you get out, if you, if things work out for you and you get a . . . have you got a job to go back to?

Christopher   Got a job in Africa.

Robert   O . . . K . . . Somewhere to stay?

Christopher   In Africa. In Uganda.

Silence.

Robert   Friends?

Christopher   In Africa.

Robert (*beat*)   Excellent.

Robert *stands.*

He hands the notes back to **Bruce***.*

Robert   Well, I think I've pretty much finished here. Doctor Flaherty?

Bruce   You're finished?

Robert   Quite finished. It's been nice chatting to you, Christopher. I sincerely hope I never clap eyes on you again, e-heh heh heh.

He shakes **Christopher***'s hand and* **Christopher** *just stares at him.*

Robert   It's a joke.

Bruce   So you're just going now?

Robert   Is that a problem? Unless you want me for anything else?

They all look at each other.

Christopher *is still holding* **Robert***'s hand.*

Christopher (*to* **Robert**)   What's up with him? (*To* **Bruce**.) What's up your arse, man?

Bruce   If you don't mind, I'd like you to stay while I ask Chris a couple more questions.

Robert   What sort of questions?

Bruce   Routine. My assessment isn't over yet.

Robert *sits reluctantly, taking his hand back.*

Robert   Why not? Fire away.

Bruce   Because, the thing is, Chris, Doctor Smith here says that you can go if you want to.

Christopher   I know. I'm going.

Bruce   But I'm wondering if you really want to?

Christopher   I want it *bad*, d'you know what I mean?

Bruce   And . . . you're *sure* you're ready. Are you sure?

Christopher   I'm cool.

Pause.

Bruce   OK. Just a couple of questions.

Christopher   Shoot.

Bruce   What's in the fruit bowl?

Christopher   How d'you mean?

Bruce   What do you see in the fruit bowl? What type of fruit do you see?

He proffers the bowl full of oranges. **Christopher** *stares at it long and hard.* **Bruce** *takes an orange from the bowl and hands it to* **Christopher** *who stares at it hard.*

He also tosses one to **Robert**.

Bruce   What's in the bowl, Chris?

Christopher   Oranges.

Bruce   Oranges, good, but what sort of oranges?

Christopher   Just oranges.

Bruce   Yes, but they're not *orange* oranges, are they?

Christopher   Nope.

Bruce   What did you tell me yesterday? Can you remember?

Pause.

Christopher   They're blue oranges.

Bruce   Blue oranges. Really?

Christopher   Bright blue.

Bruce   Peel one. See what's inside.

They wait as **Christopher** *peels the orange, holds it up.*

Bruce   What colour is it inside?

Pause.

Chris?

Christopher   It's blue.

Bruce   So the skin is blue – and even underneath the skin it's the same – it's blue?

Christopher   That's correct. Completely blue.

Pause.

It's bad. It's a bad orange. Don't eat it.

Pause.

I mean, my God! Ha ha. What is it? 'Black magic'?

Bruce   Voodoo.

Christopher   Voodoo! Oh no. *Spooky.* D'you know what I mean? It's – it's – it's *nuts.*

Bruce   'Spooky'.

Christopher   Spooky. 'Yikes!'

Bruce 'Yikes' indeed . . .

Christopher 'This bad nigga dude we got doing his voodoo again.'

Pause.

My dad, right, my dad, that's his favourite fruit. Oranges. *Orange* oranges, though. D'you know what I mean?

Bruce Who is your father, Chris? Chris?

Pause.

Christopher *eats a segment of orange.*

Bruce Who is your father?

Christopher How d'you mean?

Bruce What's his name?

Christopher I already told you.

Bruce Tell me again. In front of Robert.

Christopher Why?

Bruce Just . . . please, Chris . . . it's a simple question.

Christopher It's difficult to answer. D'you know what I mean?

Bruce No I don't. Why?

Christopher If I ask you who your father is nobody gives a shit. With me it's front-page news. D'you understand?

Bruce No, I don't understand. Why is it front-page news?

Christopher Cos of who he is.

Robert Who is he?

Christopher I'm not telling you.

Bruce (This is ridiculous.) Look. Please. Help me out here.

Christopher   You want *me* to help *you*? Now you want me to do your job.

Robert   If you can't tell us who he is – it'll be tricky for us to send you home. You will have to stay here. Do you understand?

Bruce   Who's your father, Chris?

Pause.

Christopher   It sounds silly.

Bruce   For Christ's sake –

Christopher   It's embarrassing.

Bruce   Chris!

Christopher   How can I say it, in all honesty, without you thinking I'm off the stick? How do I know it won't incriminate me, d'you know what I'm saying?

Robert   It won't incriminate you. We promise.

Christopher   Oh you 'promise'? Well, in that case, I feel a whole lot better.

Bruce   Please . . . just do this one thing for me. For me.

Pause.

Christopher   My father . . . my dad . . . was a very important man.

Pause.

Believe it or not . . . my dad . . . is former Ugandan President His Excellency Idi Amin.

Bruce   Fabulous –

Christopher   And if he knew where I was now I would not want to be you.

Bruce   Y – Chris –

Christopher   I would not want to be you.
Because The Man Does Not Fuck About, d'you understand
what I'm saying?
He will *digest* you.
He will juice you and squirt you out of his arse like a
motherfucking firehose, into the sewers for the bats and the
fish.
They don't call him 'The Butcher of the Bush' for nothing.
Believe.

Silence.

Robert   Fine . . . OK . . .

Christopher   What else d'you want to know?

Robert   Well –

Christopher   He got forty-three children and a hundred
grandchildren. He's a family man. He's a Muslim. He lives in
Saudi Arabia. In exile. 'Cept when he goes on holiday to
Paris. Every day he takes a delivery of East African oranges
from the airport. Reminds him of old times.
He drives a Chevrolet and has a talent for the accordion. A
lot of exiles drive Mercedes but he don't like to draw
attention to his self.

Robert   I see . . .

Christopher   He kicked my mum out of Uganda cos she's
from Zaire. He kicked out all the foreigners. D'you know
what I mean? I'm not proud of it. It's just the way he was.
Old-fashioned.

Pause.

Robert   'Old . . . fashioned'. Mm . . .

Pause.

Your mother is from Zaire, you say?

Christopher   You don't believe me, do you?

Robert   When was this?

Christopher   1974. Before I was born.

Robert   *Before* you were born?

Christopher   I was *conceived*. That's why she had to go. He couldn't father a foreigner. It's obvious.

Bruce *and* **Robert** *stare at each other.*

Christopher   He's got another wife in Haringey who runs a chippy. Got closed down for bad hygiene, d'you know what I mean?

Bruce   You can go back to your ward now. Chris? I'll see you later.

Christopher   But –

Bruce   It's over now.

Christopher   We finished?

Bruce   We're finished for today, yes.

Christopher   What did I say?

Robert   Absolutely nothing.

Christopher   Did I pass?

Bruce *just smiles.*

Christopher   Now you're not saying anything. That's no good.

Bruce   You have nothing to worry about.

Christopher   I don't, yeah?

Bruce   No. You're going to be fine.

Christopher   I'm still going home, right?

Pause.

I'm still going home, yeah?

Pause.

I'm . . . I'm still going home?

Robert   Shhhh . . . OK? Just relax.

Pause.

Christopher   But . . . I'm –

Robert   Shhh.

Pause.

Christopher   I'm –

Robert (*waving a finger*)   Uh. Uh-uh.

Pause.

Christopher   But I'm still going home, aren't I?

Robert   Of course you are.

Bruce   Chris? I'll speak to you later. Go back to your ward now.

Christopher   But I'm still going home, yeah?

Robert   Yes.

Bruce *takes back the remains of the orange,* **Christopher** *gets up and shuffles out.*

Robert *takes the remains of the orange from* **Bruce** *and eats a segment.*

Robert   Very interesting.

Bruce   Happy?

Robert   'Le Monde est Bleu comme une Orange'.

Bruce   What?

Robert   It's a poem by Paul Éluard. He was a French surrealist.

Bruce   You don't say.

Robert   'The World is as Blue as an Orange'. (*Beat.*) It's an analogy.

Bruce   Classic hallucinatory behaviour.

Robert   Or is it a simile?

Bruce   Already he's building a system of logic around it . . . his '*father*' who loves oranges de da de da de da.

Robert   Hypomania. Brief psychotic episode requiring short-term hospital treatment and a course of antipsychotics when he goes home. Simple.

Bruce   What if it isn't? What if it's just the tip of the iceberg?

Robert   Is he hearing voices? Auditory hallucinations?

Bruce   Not yet.

Robert   Is he seeing things – other than blue oranges?

Bruce   Isn't this enough?

Robert (*shrugs*)   For some reason he wants to see blue instead of orange. Neurotics do it all the time. They see what they want to see, not what they really see. Maybe he knows the poem.

Bruce   You're joking, aren't you?

Robert   Entirely serious. There's a lot of French speakers in Central Africa. His mother could have read it him as a child. It planted an image in his mind. When he's not a hundred per cent that image presents itself.

Bruce   You are joking.

Robert   There's a Tintin book. *Tintin and the Blue Oranges*. It's about a 'mad professor' who invents an orange which will grow in the Sahara. Only trouble is it's bright blue and tastes salty. Tintin was banned in the Belgian Congo. They thought he was a communist. But in colonial Uganda the notoriety no doubt made Tintin a 'must read' for the bourgeoisie. He was

a cultural icon and a symbol of middle-class insurrection. A
delusion waiting to happen.
BPD with Delusion.

Bruce   Are you making this up?

Robert *shakes his head.*

Bruce   Surely, you must agree, there's something terribly
wrong here. Surely we have a responsibility to . . .

Robert   A responsibility to let him out. Level 2. Prescribe
medication, CPN twice weekly.

Bruce   He won't take medication, you know that, they
never do.

Robert   That's what we have CPNs for. Just till he's back
on his feet.

Bruce   He needs looking after.

Robert   Maybe he does, maybe he doesn't.
Maybe he really does have some connection with Idi Amin.
Jesus Christ-on-a-mountain-bike. The man was spawning
offspring all over the shop.

Bruce   You can't be serious.

Robert   Maybe I am.

Bruce   Oh for God's sake.

Robert   OK, calm down.

*He paces and wipes his hands on his shirt, rubs his hands together, talks
with a mouthful.*

Now (*clears his throat*) for what it's worth, it's quite possible he's
heard some family story, handed down through the
generations, some apocryphal story, maybe Idi Amin came to
town, to the village, de da de da de da, Chinese whispers, it's
just gathered importance, gained in stature and now he
believes this. It happens. Read my manuscript.

Bruce   What manuscript?

Robert   It's a continuation of my PhD really. It's not finished. There's a chapter missing – something rather complex and enigmatic – a certain *je ne sais quoi* although I can't think what.
Seriously. I think there's something in it.

Bruce   I think there's something in feng shui, Doctor, but I wouldn't do a PhD in it.

Robert   As your supervisor I wouldn't have it any other way.

Bruce   I read your PhD. 'Cultural Antecedent and Cultural Specificity in Connection with a Delusional Belief System'. Enables us to understand the origins of delusion. African tribesmen develop delusions about sorcerers; Westerners develop delusions about the Spice Girls and extraterrestrials. The specifics of Christopher's cultural background are that his mother once lived in Uganda: he's got a delusion about a Ugandan dictator she no doubt talked about. You're saying he's not sick, it's a cultural thing.

Robert   I'm saying he's not mad. There's a difference.

Pause.

Do you know what happened to his mother in Uganda? Do you know whether she was raped by soldiers after the military coup? By Idi Amin himself? She could have been a journalist or a cook at State House for all you know. Have you asked her?

Bruce   That's not possible.

Robert   Why not?

Bruce   I can't trace her. We think she lives in Feltham.

Robert   Where in Feltham?

Bruce   Nobody seems to have an address.

Robert   Find her. It might not all be true – but then again it might.

Can you imagine the ramifications of that?
This is precisely what I'm getting at in my research.

Bruce   What are you talking about? You can't use him for research.

Robert   Why not? Why ever not? Think about it.
There is more mental illness amongst the Afro-Caribbean population in London than any other ethnic grouping.
Why?
Is it the way we're diagnosing it? Is it us? Is it them? What's causing it? What's the answer? What's the cure?
There's no 'cure' for schizophrenia.
No 'cure' for psychosis.
Only *palliative drugs*.
But what if it *isn't* psychosis? Wouldn't that be a relief? What if there is a cure? *Cognitive* therapy. *Minimal* medication.
A 'cure' for 'black psychosis'.
Imagine it.
The Holy Grail.
And imagine if the fucker who found it was . . . us.

Silence.

Bruce   'A Cure for Black Psychosis'.

Robert   Figuratively speaking.

Bruce   You're being 'whimsical' again?

Robert (*shaking his head*)   An end to palliatives. No more 'dated toxic crud'.

Bruce   OK. Say it is true. It's all true. Christopher is Idi Amin's son. And he's schizophrenic. It's both. Had you thought of that?

Pause.

Kind of blows your theory out of the water, doesn't it?

Silence.

Robert OK, look. I'm merely pointing out that sometimes our analysis is *ethnocentric*: in this case you are evaluating the situation according to your own specific cultural criteria.

Bruce 'Ethnocentric'?

Robert Our colonial antecedents are latent and barely suppressed. We are intuitively suspicious because of our cultural background.
For example, on the way back from the rugby the other night we stopped at the off-licence for a bottle of wine. I noticed that the Pakistani gentleman behind the counter said neither Please nor Thank you. I had to ask myself, is he just *like* that – is he just *rude*? Or is it because there is no such thing as Please and Thank you in Urdu – is it not customary in his culture?

Bruce What are you talking about? He always says Please and Thank you.

Robert OK, fine. So perhaps I should ask myself, Is it me? What are *my* cultural expectations?

Bruce Look, after the rugby, everybody goes in there, all the rugger buggers, pissy drunk and *they* don't say Please and Thank you –

Robert Nevertheless, we must guard against our ethnocentricity.

Bruce I don't think I like the direction this is heading.

Robert The point is, this is my *province*, Doctor.
That's why you asked me here.
Because I know how many beans make five.
I am, as they say, an 'expert'.
I am Senior Consultant and I am here to be 'consulted'.
I am not here to be 'bounced off'.
To 'run it up the flag pole and see who salutes'.
I'm here because 'I know'.

Bruce But . . . with the greatest respect, Doctor Smith, you don't. He's *my* patient . . . so . . . really . . .

Robert   OK, fine. Whatever. Discharge him. Next case.

Pause.

Bruce   But –

Robert   We can skin this cat as artfully as we like.
However, in the opinion of this highly experienced
Department Head, Doctor Flaherty, what we have here is No
Beds and, more importantly, a patient who has No Need of a
Bed.

Bruce   But I think –

Robert   What I 'think' is that you think too much.
What I think is that you should let me do the thinking.
Now if you don't mind, I'm very busy.

Robert *goes to the door.*

Bruce   But . . . you're saying . . . what you're really saying is
Christopher's . . . unable to distinguish between realistic and
utterly unrealistic notions because . . . what . . . ? Because he's
. . . ?

Robert   BPD. Case closed.

Bruce   It's because he's b –

Robert   BPD. Goodbye, Doctor.

Bruce   Because he's black?

Robert *sighs, clenches his teeth. Walks back into the room.*

Robert *(icily)*   I'm saying where he comes from it is almost
certainly not an unrealistic notion. Where we come from, it
evidently is. Get it?

Bruce   But he comes from Shepherd's Bush.

Robert   He sees himself as African. And we don't say
'black' any more –

Bruce   Yes we do –

Robert   We say 'Afro-Caribbean'.

Bruce   Where does the Caribbean come into it?

Robert   All right, he's 'African'.

Bruce   From Shepherd's Bush.

Robert   I'm not going to quibble over this twaddle.

Bruce   'Twaddle'?

Robert   I'm not going to squabble. His 'origins' are in Africa.

Bruce   How far back are you going?

Robert   And for the last time I'll remind you that you are under my supervision, you are my subordinate, and your tone is beginning to sound dangerously insubordinate if not nakedly insulting.

Bruce   I'm sorry . . . but –

Robert   Do you know what most young doctors would do to have me as Supervisor? I mean, normal ones . . . the smart ones . . . what they'd do to know they have a future. To have a shot at becoming Consultant? They'd *lick my anus*.

Silence.

(But that's beside the point . . .)

He goes to the door and looks out.
Comes back. Sits.

Now. Do you want me to recommend your consultancy at this hospital or don't you?

Bruce   Of course.

Robert   Then act like a professional. Act like a representative of the Royal College of Psychiatrists.

Bruce   But I'm *not* a –

Robert   Do you want to be? Mm? Now. Pull yourself together. Try not to be so wet behind the ears. Otherwise I'm taking you off this case.

Bruce   You can't take me off this case.

Robert   I'll assign a CPN and discharge him myself.

Bruce   If you do I'll appeal to the Authority.

Robert   I am the Authority. (Just between you and me.)

Bruce   But . . . um . . . with respect, it's it's it's it's what I believe in.

Robert   Well, you know, Doctor, with respect, that isn't good enough.

Bruce   It's not good enough that I do what I believe is right?

Robert   That's right. It's naive.

Bruce   *Naive?*

Robert   That's right. You're naive. And you're beginning to get on my *wick*.

Silence.

Bruce   Why won't you listen to me?

Robert   What? 'Listen to you'? To you? It's not my job to listen to you. It's your job to . . . oh for goodness' sake . . .

Pause.

OK. All right. Listen.
Let me join up some of the dots for you.
Let me do some of the maths for you:
Schizophrenia is the worst pariah.
One of the last great taboos.
People don't understand it.
They don't want to understand it.
It scares them.
It depresses them.
It is not treatable with glamorous and intriguing wonderdrugs like Prozac or Viagra.
It isn't newsworthy.

It isn't curable.

It isn't heroin or Ecstasy.

It is not the preserve of rock stars and supermodels and hip young authors.

It is not a topic of dinner-party conversation.

Organised crime gets better press.

They make *movies* about junkies and alcoholics and gangsters and men who drink too much, fall over and beat their woman until bubbles come out of her nose, but schizophrenia, my friend, is just not in the phone book.

Bruce   Then we must change that.

Robert   . . . And they . . . *what?*

Bruce   Then we must change that.

Robert   'Change'. Hmm. Well . . . the thing is, you can't change that. D'you see? I can't. Seriously.

The Authority – the rest of the Board, not even me – they will question your expertise. They will wonder why you got so upset about it. They will wonder whether or not this case has a 'deeper personal significance' to you and they will undermine you at every turn and then they will screw you. As sure as eggs are fucking eggs.

Bruce   A 'deeper personal . . .'?

Robert   People will question your mental *wellness*.

Silence.

They'll say you're mad.

And then they'll say *I'm* mad for supervising you and allowing my department to disintegrate so.

Bruce   Well, if you don't want to supervise me . . . if you've changed your mind . . . you only have to say.

Robert   Not at all. This is a 'Teaching Hospital' and I am here to teach.

Bruce   W . . . was it Saturday? Did I say something after the rugby?

Robert   Look. I'm not the big bad wolf. I'm not trying to
undermine your decision and I certainly don't want to release
Christopher if he isn't ready. I *care*. And I know you care. All
I'm saying is sometimes one can care *too much*. One can have
too much Empathy – Understanding – an *overweening*
Compassion. You try to be all things to all men: Doctor.
Friend. A *reasonable* man. We all want to be *reasonable* men.
Eh? Bruce? Please. Now. Am I not your friend?

Pause.

Aren't we friends?

Bruce *slowly nods.*

Robert   Sleep on it.
Let me conduct my own assessment. We can reconvene in the
morning and all decide together. Eh? I'll talk to him tonight. I
promise you I won't be partisan.

Bruce   OK. Fine. Whatever you say.

Robert   Don't look so gloomy. Just wait till you're a
consultant. Think of that loft conversion.

Bruce   Robert . . .

Robert   Bruce . . . Bruce . . . Bruce . . .
You have it all to look forward to.
Trust me.
I want what you want. I really do.
I believe in what you believe in.
I'm On Your Side.

Blackout.

Act Two

That night. **Robert** *and* **Christopher** *sit facing each other across the table. A reading light is the only light.*

Robert *takes a cigarette from his pack and lights it.* **Christopher** *takes a cigarette from behind his ear and* **Robert** *lights it. They exhale.*

Robert   Listen listen listen listen.

Pause.

Listen.

Pause.

We all have these thoughts. It's perfectly natural. Even I have them. Yes. Me. Some days I get home from work, from a long night in the hospital, visiting, ward rounds, nothing untoward, nothing terrible, a few cross words with a colleague, some silly argument, I get home and I get in the door and I *slump*. All the life drains out of me. I think . . . Why Am I Doing This? Eh? What's in it for me? A table at the Ivy if I use the right prefix. A seminar in Norway. Some spotty young registrar takes me to the rugby and hangs on my every word. Big deal. And there are times, when I look across at this professor and that professor turning up to work in a new *Jag*, he's just come back from La Rochelle, he's off to play a round of golf at his thousand-pound-a-year golf club, have a drink at his jolly old Mayfair club, posh dinners with drug company reps, knighthoods, appearances on Radio Four n'ha ha ha . . .
And I think . . . How do they do that?
What, are they 'experts' or something?
I Want To Be Professor!
What do they do that I don't?
And the answer is:
Who *cares*? That's *their* life. Nevertheless, I feel small and I think my life adds up to nothing. And I have to keep reminding myself: Why not? Why not think these things? It's

not greedy, it's not covetous. It's *human*. It's me being a
human being. And it applies to us all. And it's my right to do
something about it. It's everybody's right to take steps.
But *killing yourself*?
Christopher?
Why?

Silence.

Everybody Feels Like This. At some point. In their life. Everybody feels that they've . . . lost out. It's the Human Condition.
The capacity to feel *disappointment*. It's what distinguishes us
from the animals. Our *disappointment*. Mm. It's true. The
capacity to grieve for lost opportunity. For the lives we *could*
have *led*. The men or women we *may* have become. It has us
in an appalling stranglehold.
And sometimes we say, Why Go On? And we want to end it
all. The hell with it. Life's a sham.
That's human too. You don't hear doggies running about
going, 'Oh that this too too solid flesh would melt.' Of course
not. Why not? They're *dogs*! It would be ridiculous. Dogs have
other talents. They can lick their own balls. A talent for
simplicity. N'ha ha ha. Do you see? Learn to cultivate a
Talent for Simplicity.

Pause.

Christopher   Learn to Lick My Balls?
That's your expert advice, yeah?

Robert   N'ha ha ha. N'ha ha ha, well . . . it might work . . .

Christopher   You're a fucking *doctor*, man.

Robert   I know, I'm joking, but you, you, you see my point.
This life is a *gift*. The food we eat, the smells we smell, the
trees, the sky, the *fecundity* of Creation . . . It's a *really lovely* gift,
and if for whatever reason you cannot see that right now,
then I'm here to Heal Your Vision. To help you. See. I
promise you, I plead with you, I *entreat* you. Take a few deep
breaths. Calm down. Think about this. You're not 'suicidal'.
It's ridiculous.

Silence.

Christopher   I don't want to go home.

Pause.

I changed my mind. I'm not going.

Robert   Christopher . . .

Christopher   I . . . I . . . I don't have a home. I'm not . . .
I'm not ready.

Robert   What happens to you when you go home?

Christopher   I told you about the Fuzz.

Robert   OK. Fine. But apart from . . . the 'Fuzz'. What else
happens to you?

Pause.

Chris?

Pause.

Christopher   People stare at me. Like they know . . . like
they know about me.
Like they know something about me that I don't know.

Robert   Such as?

Christopher   Eh?

Robert   What could they know that you don't know?

Christopher   I don't know. They hate me. They think
I'm bad.

Robert   Which people?

Christopher   Eh?

Robert   Who are these people who . . . think you're bad?

Christopher   I hear noises. At night. Outside my window.
Sometimes I hear . . . talking. People talking about me.

Robert   Talking about you?

Christopher　Laughing sometimes.

Robert　And you've no idea who it is?

Christopher　No idea. Sometimes I hear machinery. Whirring. Like a . . . a strange droning noise. And beeping. A strange beeping noise. Very loud.

Robert　It's the dustbin men.

Christopher　On Saturdays and Sundays?

Robert　Builders. OK? We're in the midst of a property boom. Interest rates are low, people are buying and building and renovating – people want more of the life gifted them. Life is Rich. People are greedy for Life.

Christopher　Not in White City they're not. 'White City'. 'South Africa Road'. Even the names are a fucking wind-up.

Robert　But you have your friends. Your *community*. People who care.

Christopher　I don't have any friends.
I try to make friends with people but it's not easy. I try to make conversation but it's not easy. Sometimes I say the wrong thing.
Actually I always say the wrong thing. I don't have a girlfriend. Who'd want me?

Pause.

Robert　Well. You'll make new friends when you get out.

Christopher　I made friends with Bruce.

Robert　You won't be alone in all this. I'll make sure of that.

Christopher　Yeah but I want double glazing. Don't talk to me about the fucking property boom. It's like living in a biscuit tin.

Pause.

Robert   Well, you know, Chris, I can't provide you with double glazing. It's not part of my remit. If you want double glazing . . .
Go to the Council. See your housing officer.

Christopher   You said you would help me.

Robert   I know, but –

Christopher   So help me –

Robert   It's –

Christopher   Help me –

Robert   It's not my job! N'ha ha ha. D'you see?

Christopher   Yeah, but what I thought was, if I moved somewhere else –

Robert   OK. There's a procedure for that. The Council will have a procedure for transferring you.

Christopher   Yeah, but I wanna go to Africa.

Robert   You want to go to Africa.

Christopher   I want to go to Africa.

Robert   Back to your roots.

Christopher   My 'roots'?

Robert   You feel you 'belong' there?

Christopher   *No*, man. I already told you. It's nice there. And and and you know I told you about my dad.

Robert   Idi Amin.

Christopher   Idi Amin Dada. That's his proper name. Idi Amin Dada.

Robert   O . . . K . . .

Pause.

Tell me about your mother. What did she do in Uganda?

Christopher She was a barmaid.

Robert A 'barmaid'. Really? In a pub?

Christopher No, in a shoe shop, innit.

Robert Where the soldiers drank?

Christopher Eh?

Robert Did many soldiers drink there?

Christopher I don't know.

Robert What I'm getting at is . . . how . . . how did your mum actually meet President Amin?

Silence.

Christopher *stares into space.*

Robert Christopher?

Christopher You wouldn't understand.

Robert Why wouldn't I understand?

Christopher You wouldn't understand.

Silence.

Robert Try me.

Christopher She was a student. He closed down the university for political reasons.

Robert She told you this?

Christopher She never talks about it – d'you know what I mean? It's personal.

Pause.

She gets upset.

Robert What did she read?

Christopher How d'you mean?

Robert What was her subject? English literature?

Christopher   How d'you mean?

Robert   What I'm getting at is, well, does she read you poetry, for example? Or plays?

Christopher   No.

Robert   What about at school? Did you read poetry at school?

Christopher   No.

Robert   Oh. OK. Fine.

Pause.

What about books? Children's books? Comics? *Tintin*? *Asterix*? She must have given you books.

Christopher   No.

Robert   Do you still see her? Christopher? D'you know where she lives?

Pause.

Chris?

Christopher   She lives in Feltham.

Robert   Do you know her address? Do you want to tell me?

Pause.

You don't want to tell me where she lives?
Why should I believe you if you can't even tell me your mother's address?

Christopher   Bruce don't believe me either but I can prove it.

Robert   You can 'prove it'?

Christopher   Yeah, man.

Robert   How?

Christopher   Why should I tell you?

Robert   Well . . . because I'm asking you to . . .

Christopher   What if I don't trust you?

Robert   Well . . . then . . . that would be a great shame.

Christopher   A shame? (*Beat.*) You think it'd be a shame, yeah?

Robert   Yeah.

Christopher   Oh.

Christopher *weighs it up.*
He produces a wallet from his pocket.
From the wallet he produces a tightly folded-up newspaper article.
He unfolds it and holds it out to **Robert**.
Robert *hesitates, then takes it and reads.*
Christopher *reads over his shoulder.*

Robert (*reading*)   'A delivery of East African oranges from the airport . . . the Butcher of the Bush . . . talent for the accordion blah blah blah . . . Forty-three children by four wives . . .'

Christopher   Five wives.

Robert   Eh?

Christopher   Five wives really. There's a fifth. A secret one.

Robert   A . . . a . . . where?

Christopher (*pointing*)   Not the one who runs a chippy. Another one. Common-law wife. Living in 'penury'.

Robert (*reading*)   'Living in . . . in Feltham.'

Christopher   In 'penury'.

Robert   'In penury . . . in Feltham.' Bugger me. How long have you had this?

Christopher   My mother gave it to me.

Robert   Bugger me.

They look at each other.

Silence.

Robert *puts his fingertips to his temples momentarily, thinking hard.*

Christopher (*pointing*)   Look. That's his photo.

Robert (*holding the article*)   Can I keep this?

Christopher   No you cannot keep that.

Robert   Please. Christopher . . . listen . . .

Christopher *snatches the article back, folds it, puts it away as he speaks.*

Christopher   I am being *harassed*. I'm in fear of my *life*. I live in *fear*. They Know Who I Am.

Robert   Who does?

Christopher   The men. Where I live. The noises. The . . . the police. It all makes sense.

Robert   They're . . . look . . . it's . . . they're just ordinary *men*. *Work* men . . . *police* men.

Christopher   Other men too. Another man. He throws bananas at me.

Robert   Bananas . . . ?

Christopher   When I'm at work. Even at work – d'you know what I mean! Big bloke with a little pointy head. Long thin arms trailing along the ground. A real knuckle-dragger. Very white skin. Hideous-looking bastard. He's the ring-leader. I see him at night. He bangs on my door. Says he's coming to get me. He says he'll do me and nobody would even notice and I believe him. There's a whole family of them. A tribe. I don't like them at all. They're a race apart. *Zombies*! The undead. Monsters!
QPR supporters.

Pause.

Robert   Football hooligans?

Christopher   On Saturdays, I seem 'em in the crowds at Loftus Road.
They come after the game. And before the game. With bananas.
With . . . with shit smeared through the letter box, not dog shit – real shit. Pissing through the letter box, fires, firestarting on the front step. It's a disgrace. They call me 'Jungle Boy'. If my dad was here he'd kill them dead. He'd monster them.
Believe.

Silence.

It's their appearance that spooks me the most. Those tiny, bony, shrunken heads. All shaved. Ugly.

Robert   D'you mean . . . Skinheads?

Christopher   *Zombies.*

Robert   What makes you think these people are . . . 'the undead'?

Christopher   They look *half* dead. It's that ghostly white skin, looks like tapioca, d'you know what I mean?

Robert   Christopher –

Christopher   Baldies. 'Baldy-Heads', that's what I call them. Baldy-Heads.

Robert   'Baldy-Heads'. I see. But . . . they're not really . . . 'Zombies', now are they? Chris? Which is it, 'Zombies' or 'Baldy-Heads'?

Pause.

There is a difference.

Christopher   D'you think it's funny?

Robert   Not in the least. It could be the difference between you staying here or you going home.

Christopher   They're *dangerous*, man. Believe. They're spooky. I could be dead tomorrow.

Robert *rubs his eyes and sighs.*

Christopher   You know the average life expectancy of the modern black male? Sixty-four years old. That's how long we got. What age do we get the pension? *Sixty-five!* It's a fucking *rip-off*, man! D'you know what I mean?

Robert   So . . . fundamentally, you don't think you're sick? Am I right?

Christopher   Yeah I'm sick. Sick and tired, man. Sick of everything. I got problems. D'you know what I'm saying?

Robert   Do you keep a diary?

Christopher   A diary? No. Do you?

Robert   You should start keeping a diary.

Christopher   I never go out.

Robert   No, a diary of what *happens*.

Christopher   Nothing ever happens, man. All day every day, nothing.

Robert   I meant, things on the estate. Concerning the letter box . . . ? OK?
Then you go to the Council, you ask to see your housing officer and you show her the diary. She can have you transferred to a different estate.

Christopher   It gets a bit lonely sometimes but –

Robert   Yes I know and that's OK. That's normal. That's human. And I'll tell you something else –

Christopher   Sometimes people scare me.

Robert   I know they do. And you know what you do when they do these things?

Christopher   What?

Robert   You laugh.

Christopher   Laugh?

Robert   When somebody hurts you, just laugh at them. You don't care. They'll soon get the message.

Pause.

Christopher   Laugh, yeah?

Robert   It drives them crazy. Really, it's a good trick.

Christopher   Oh I get you. Laugh. Really.
HA HA HA HA HA. HA HA HA HA HA. 'Laugh and the whole world laughs with you.'
AND THEN THEY LOCK YOU UP!
What the fuck are you on about, man? D'you know what I mean? Pull yourself together!

Robert   OK. Cry. Do handstands. Express Yourself. Just Don't Take It Personally.

Christopher   'Express myself'. And who are you: 'Professor Groovy'?

Robert   Strictly speaking it's 'Doctor Groovy'. N'ha ha ha ha. N'ha ha ha. See? You can do it.

Silence.

No. You're quite right. I'm sorry. But, you see, the thing is, Chris, I don't think that you are ill and I want you to try to settle down somewhere.

Christopher   I think Bruce is right. I'm not ready. I don't wanna go.

Robert   OK . . . well . . . did he actually say that to you, did he?

Christopher   He asked me if I was sure.

Robert   And you said you were, didn't you?

Christopher   Yeah, but I was lying. D'you know what I mean?

Pause.

Robert   You were *lying*.

Christopher   I was lying.

Robert   Why?

Christopher   Cos I wanted to get out of this place.

Robert   Aha! 'The truth will out.' You 'wanted to get out of this place'. You did. It's true.

Christopher   But now I don't.

Robert   Yes you do.

Christopher   No I don't.

Robert   I think you do.

Christopher   I fucking don't, man.

Robert   You do and I'm going to continue to suggest to you that you do whether your conscious mind likes it or not.

Pause.

You see, until your *conscious* mind catches up with what your *subconscious* mind wants . . . and *knows*, which is that you, quote, 'want to get out of here', unquote, you're never going to get better. And you're never going to get out of here.

Christopher   I'm never . . . ?

Robert   Nope. Never. You'll be in hospital – this hospital or some other hospital somewhere – in and out of hospital for the rest of your life.
For the rest of your life.

Pause.

Christopher   Now I'm scared.

Robert   Sure. Of course you are. And I think that that's right. I think if you weren't nervous, you wouldn't be human.

Christopher   I didn't say I was nervous.

Robert   Well . . . I think you are.

Christopher   Oh man. What am I gonna do?

Robert   I've just told you what to do.

Christopher   Uh?

Robert   I just told you what you should do.

Christopher *stares into space.*

Robert   Chris . . . ? The Council . . . ? Your housing officer –

Christopher   He said I could stay. Doctor Flaherty said –

Robert   You know what I think? I think that you think you are scared. And that's all it is, a thought. And I think that it's not your thought.

Christopher   What d'you mean?

Robert   I think that someone else's thoughts have scared you.

Christopher   You think . . . I'm thinking someone else's thoughts?

Pause.

Whose thoughts?

Robert   I'm saying . . . look . . . Maybe Doctor Flaherty 'projected' his fears of letting you go home on to you and now they're *your* fears.
I'm saying maybe, just maybe Doctor Flaherty . . . unconsciously put his thoughts in your head.

Christopher   He put his thoughts in my head. In my head . . . ?

Robert   Look, this morning, you were ready to go home. You were so excited. You couldn't wait. You wanted coffee, you had your bags packed, wahey, it was all happening for you. Remember?

Christopher   Mm . . .

Robert   So what's changed? What's new, my friend? Eh?

Pause.

Nothing. You had your bags packed.

Pause.

Nothing has changed. You're going home. Stop thinking about it. Just do it.

Christopher   But, see, the thing is, I got the impression, I got the impression from Doctor Flaherty –

Robert   What? Did he say something? What did he say?

Christopher   No, but I got the impression –

Robert   Well, did you read his mind?

Christopher *stares.*

Silence.

Robert   OK, forget that, bad idea. But but but . . . what I'm saying is How Do You Know? Because really: he *wants* you to go too. He wants rid of you. I should know.

Christopher   He wants rid of me?

Robert   Yes. He's had enough of you, my friend, we all have, don't jolly well . . . outstay your welcome! N'huh huh huh. Go. Be free.

Pause.

N'huh huh huh. D'you see?

Pause.

I'm trying to help you.

Christopher   I read his mind?

Robert   I said to forget that.

Christopher   He wants rid of me?

Robert   I'm joking. It's a joke!

Christopher   The oranges are blue.

Silence.

Remember he asked me what colour the orange was?

Robert   Mm.

Christopher   And I said it was blue. It was. I *saw* that.

Pause.

Bright blue. Virtually glowing.

Robert   You've had a psychotic episode. Things will be a bit strange for a while. Nothing more insidious.

Christopher   'A bit strange'? They were blue.

Robert   We will give you medication for that.

Christopher   I'm seeing things.

Robert   OK OK OK, look. You're not.

Christopher   What?

Robert   You're not seeing things. I think . . . all right . . . I think you wanted so badly to stay here, subconsciously, that you thought you saw things, or you said you saw things . . .

Christopher   You saying I was lying? *Me?*

Robert   N . . . I'm saying you were lying. Yes.

Christopher   Well, I think *you're* lying.

Robert   Because you wanted to stay here. But, you see, if you do stay here, if we give you what we call a Section 3, you will stay here Indefinitely.

Christopher   How d'you mean?

Robert   We can keep you for up to six months. We can keep you, more or less, for as long as we like.

Pause.

Christopher   You're prolly not even a proper doctor.

Robert   Well . . . n'ha . . . I can assure you, Chris, I am a 'proper doctor'.

Christopher   Prove it.

Robert   I don't have to prove it.

Christopher   Well, that's not fair, is it? What about my job? D'you know what I mean? I got a job to go to. On a fruit stall. In the market. I *sell* oranges.

Pause.

Robert   You sell oranges? (I didn't know that . . .)

Christopher   It's true. What am I supposed to tell the customers? I'm in no condition to sell fruit, d'you know what I'm saying? Same as I say, I got problems.

Pause.

Robert   Well. OK. In fact, as I remember, and correct me if I'm wrong: *First*, Doctor Flaherty *told* you it wasn't orange. The first thing he said was: 'It's not an orange orange.' What does that tell you?
You spontaneously made what's called a 'common association'. You may just have easily said Red.
It's harmless.

Christopher   It means something.

Robert   What does it mean?

Christopher   It's a sign. Cos nobody believes me but I think it proves it.
He likes oranges. Every day a shipment from Nairobi. I just

proved that. I come in here, first thing I see, oranges! They
turn blue. A *signal*.

Pause.

Robert   OK, look . . . we don't have to concern ourselves
with these things now.

Christopher   Yeah, but I'm worried now. I got the fear.

Robert   There's nothing to be afraid of.

Christopher   You don't know that.

Robert   I do, yes, I do. Because. Two reasons. I'll tell you
then you'll promise to stop fretting about them, OK? Two
things.
One: We can sort these things out when you get home. It's
unfair for you to be here while we answer those questions.
They are not life-threatening.
They are not a danger to you.
You are not a danger to yourself.
You'll be seeing me once a month and you'll be quite safe
and so now I want you to forget all about it.

Christopher   Seeing *you*?

Robert   If I take over your case, yes. That might happen.

Christopher   Why should I see you?

Robert   Because it's what I think is best. Because . . . it
would be a 'shame' if you didn't.

Pause.

Christopher   Yeah, but I wanna see Doctor Flaherty.

Robert   I'd be better.

Christopher   Uh-huh.

Pause.

What's the other thing? You said there was two.

Robert   The *second* thing is . . .

Pause.

Doctor Flaherty . . .
Bruce . . . is somewhat *unorthodox* in his approach. What he's
suggesting by keeping you in here is, you have to understand,
a little unorthodox. We don't do that any more if we can help
it. We want you out there.
We want you to go *home*. D'you see?

Christopher   Yeah, but he's worried, that's all.

Robert   I know, and that's because, you see, Bruce, Bruce,
see, Bruce is a little, as we say in the trade, He's a Tee-Pee
and a Wig-Wam.

Pause.

He's Too Tense.

Pause.

Heh heh. No I'm kidding. But he is . . . you know, he's just a,
you know, *I'm* the Head of Department. I'm the Boss. I'm the
Big Cheese.

Pause.

The Top Banana.

Pause.

OK, this is very delicate. It's not something we know an awful
lot about. But it's my specific field of research, I'm writing a
book on it as a matter of fact.

Christopher   You're writing a book? Really? You're really
writing a book?

Robert   Well . . . I blush to the toes of my shoes to admit
but . . .

Christopher   What's it about?

Robert   Well . . . it's about . . . it's about psychosis
diagnosis. In . . . people like you.

Christopher   People like me, yeah?

Robert   You see, I believe there may be a cognitive therapy which we can substitute for the drug palliatives normally associated with psychosis.
My 'assertion' is this:
There is a Cultural Specificity to the apparently delusionary nature of some of your beliefs.
There are Antecedents for some of the beliefs you hold.
'Cultural Specificity and Cultural Antecedent or Schizophrenia'.
You see? '*Or* Schizophrenia'. Not 'And'. That's what it's called.

Pause.

Christopher   What does Doctor Flaherty think about it?

Robert   Well . . . uh . . . he hasn't read it yet.

Christopher   I meant about me seeing you.

Robert   Oh well . . . OK . . . well, the thing is . . . see . . .

Pause.

Doctor Flaherty isn't in possession of the full facts.

Christopher   Why not?

Robert   Because he's not an authority. I'm an authority. He isn't.

Pause.

Because there are things you do and things you believe which he, within his culture, can only recognise as Insanity.

Pause.

Which I personally believe, for what it's worth, is rather narrow-minded . . . it's what some people call 'Culturally Oppressive'.

Christopher   Insanity.

Robert   It means he has a tendency to overlook, in our discussions at any rate, your cultural identity.

Pause.

It's nothing . . . it's no big deal . . . it's an oversight, that's all. It's a vastly complex subject. People get things wrong.

Christopher   What did he say?

Robert   OK, look. I don't want you to take this the wrong way because I don't think he meant it in a pejorative sense . . . I'm quite sure . . . but it indicates a gap in his knowledge which I'm trying to *redress*.

Christopher   What did he say?

Robert   Well . . . well . . . since you asked . . . I think he has a very real fear that . . . our response to you is weighted by our response to your colour. I personally feel that *should* be the case; it *should* be a factor in your treatment and that we shouldn't overlook such a thing. Otherwise what happens, in institutions such as this, there develops what's termed 'ethnocentricity'; which ordinarily is fairly harmless but in certain instances is not far off . . . well . . . it is the progenitor of 'cultural oppression', which in turn leads to what we call 'institutionalised racism'.

Christopher   Racism?

Robert   Yes. And the danger is that in a sense you maybe end up, in a sense, being 'punished' for the colour of your skin. (*Beat.*) For your ethnicity and your attendant cultural beliefs. (*Beat.*) You are sectioned and locked up when you shouldn't be. (*Beat.*) Because you're 'black'.

Silence.

Christopher   I'm being *punished*?

Robert   Maybe that's too strong a term but but but –

Christopher   Because I'm *black*?

Robert   Well, you see, the system is *flawed*. People of ethnic minority are not well catered for, it's a well-known fact. I've just expressed it clumsily –

Christopher   He said that? I'm locked up because I'm black?

Christopher *stands abruptly*.

Robert   No, that's not what was said. Let me finish –

Christopher   Where is he?

Robert   OK, calm down.

Christopher   The fuck does that mean?

Robert   Chris Chris Chris Chris –

Christopher   He really said that? It's cos I'm black?

Christopher *heads for the door and* **Robert** *rushes around and blocks his way, trying to hold him back*.

Robert (*struggling with him*)   Look, listen, look, listen, look, listen, look, listen, look, listen . . .

Pause.

Chris, my dear dear fellow, just sit down and listen for one moment please.
Our colonial antecedents are latent and barely suppressed –

Christopher   What shit!

He paces angrily.

Robert   This really is a storm in a teacup.

Christopher   Punished by who?

Robert   Chris, please, sit down. Sit down. Come on now. I implore you.

Christopher *sits and thinks, stares, quiet*.

Christopher   Who am I being punished by?

Robert   Well, by, by, by the *system*. The system tends to punish without meaning to.

Christopher   That's why I see things? I'm being punished?

Robert   No . . . Chris –

Christopher   That's why I hear things? These *mental* . . . *fucking* . . . the noises I hear . . . the *fear* –

Robert   What he said was –

Christopher   You said I'm not thinking my own thoughts –

Robert   No –

Christopher   Well, whose thoughts am I thinking?

Robert   Nobody –

Christopher   Doctor Flaherty's . . . ?

Robert   OK, let's not get off the track –

Christopher   He smokes too much *drugs*, man, d'you know what I mean? He likes his puff. I can tell.

Silence.

Robert   Sorry . . . you said? About . . . dr . . . ?

Christopher   He *told* me I should go back out there and *score* some puff, man. Why did he say that? Because I'm black?

Robert   O . . . K . . . but . . . I'm sure . . .

Pause.

'Puff'. For *him* . . . ? Or . . . for . . . ?

Christopher   He goes he goes he goes, If I was only in here to get drugs I'd come to the wrong place. He said the drugs out there, right, were more *fun*.

Robert   I see, well . . . I see . . . well. (*Beat.*) When was this?

Christopher   Earlier. Before you got here.

Robert   Just before or . . . some time before?

Christopher   Just before. This morning.

Robert   Oh.

Pause.

What else did he say?

Christopher   He said it was 'voodoo'. That's why I'm here. Voodoo. Remember?

Robert   W . . . ell . . .

Christopher   And he lied to me. He said he was letting me out when he was just gonna keep me in here longer just like you said, man. He lied to me.

Pause.

And and and he keeps looking at me funny.

Pause.

Can I have a cup of coffee now?

Blackout.

Act Three

Next afternoon. **Bruce** *and* **Christopher** *sit facing each other; the bowl of oranges is on the table between them.*

Bruce *has a report in front of him and is reading from it.*

Christopher *is smoking a cigarette and staring into space.*

Bruce 'He ordered the patient to peel the orange . . .' I didn't *order* you.

He reads.

'. . . establishing that it was the same under the skin. That the flesh was the same colour as the skin.'
OK, I *suggested*, Chris, I *prompted*, and maybe I shouldn't have but, you know, it's not as if this was the first time, was it? You don't need my help to start . . . (*reading*) seeing things . . .

He reads.

Pause.

Do you really believe this? Do you really think I . . . what? I'm . . . 'Provocative, unorthodox, patronising . . .'? And . . . 'Possibly *on drugs* . . .'? I mean, this is . . . this just . . . I've never heard anything so ridiculous in my life!

He reads.

'He snatched away a cup of coffee given to the patient by the consultant . . . He used the pejorative epithet "nigger".'

Silence.

I did not, um, my God, I didn't use the epithet . . . nnn . . .

He stares.

I did not call you a . . . um, um, um, a . . . I didn't say that.

Christopher Say what?

Bruce Would you please put that out? Christopher? The cigarette.

Christopher *mashes out the cigarette on the table.*

Bruce   I, I, I, didn't call you a, a, a, um, a . . . a . . . (*beat*) 'nigger'.

Christopher   You said 'uppity nigga'. You did. Deny.

Bruce   Only because *you* did. My God! It was a quote!

Christopher   Yeah, but you shouldn'ta said it.

Bruce   Oh, so so so only you can say it?

Christopher   It's not polite.

Bruce   I know it isn't and, um . . .
I'm sorry, excuse me . . .
I feel sick . . .

He steadies himself.

Pause.

Do, do you really think I meant it? Do you really think I meant to 'provoke' you? I was giving vent to 'racist' proclivities?

Christopher   Look. I don't know. I don't know. I just want to go home.

Bruce   What is wrong with you?
Are you out of your mind?
Have you been drinking?

Robert *appears in the doorway, listening.*
He enters and sits down.

Robert   You asked to see me.

Bruce   We have a meeting.

Pause.

We agreed to meet today. The three of us. Unless you know of something that could have happened to change that.

Robert   I'm on the Authority, Doctor Flaherty, of course I know.

Pause.

There was a Management Hearing this morning.

Bruce   Yes I know. How convenient.

Robert *shrugs.*

Bruce   So. Where do we go from here?

Robert   Well, you know, actually, what I think is that you and I need to be alone together.

Bruce   OK. Uh. Christopher, would you mind coming back in . . . ?

He checks his watch.

Christopher   But I've just packed.

Bruce   That's all right. Just go back to your ward and I'll send for you.

Christopher   But I've just –

Bruce   Please, Chris.

Christopher   But we –

Bruce   Please?

Christopher   But . . . I'm getting out today. My twenty-eight –

Bruce   OK, look –

Christopher   My twenty-eight –

Bruce   Chris –

Christopher   My twenty –

Bruce   I know but –

Christopher   My –

Bruce   All right!

Pause.

Not now. *Later.* I'll send for you.

Christopher   I already packed.

Bruce   I know.

Christopher *stands and exits.*

Robert   I know exactly what you're thinking and before you say anything I want you to know it was nothing to do with me. (*Beat.*) I mean, whatever he said to the *rest* of the Authority . . . (*Beat.*) I had no idea that he'd done this when I went into that Management Hearing this morning. I knew he wanted to make a complaint to the Authority – I tried to talk him out of it. That's the last I knew of it.

Bruce   But you 'are the Authority'.

Robert   OK . . . I'm a *representative* at *Management Hearings*. One of many.

Bruce   But yesterday you said you 'are the Authority'.

Robert   Only sometimes . . . sometimes it's me, yes, who . . . whoever is . . . *everybody* runs it. It's a different person each week depending on . . . it's more of a *committee* than a, than a . . .

Bruce   The point is . . . have you read this?

Pause.

Robert   Of course I've read it.

Bruce   Don't tell me. You've read it because: you wrote it?

Robert   Of course I didn't write it. What kind of bastard do you take me for?

Pause.

Bruce (*reading*)   'After some initial difficulty following the patient's interpretation of events, the Authority reached a consensus that if the said orange was indeed to be viewed as blue for the purposes of the analogy . . .' For the purposes of . . . ?

He gives **Robert** *a look.*

Bruce   '. . . then clearly as a blue-skinned orange it was indeed in the minority given that other citruses are ordinarily orange, yellow or . . .'

He gives **Robert** *a look.*

Bruce   'By asking the patient to peel the "minority" orange . . . and declaring the insides of the orange to be of equally unusual colouring, the house officer seems to have implied . . .'
What did you *say* to him?

Robert   I didn't say anything.

Bruce *reads.*

Bruce   'The Authority reached a consensus.' How?
Did everybody think of the the the stupidest things they could think of and then put them all in a hat?
By playing a drinking game?
Small children wouldn't come up with this.
Monkeys could do better using *sign language.*
For God's sake!

Robert   'Monkeys'.

Bruce   Yes.

Robert   Is that another analogy?

Bruce *stares.*

Robert   It's too easy to misinterpret, Bruce. You really have to be more careful.

Bruce   Well. Do you agree with 'the Authority'?

Robert   I rather think I should remain impartial on this one. Besides, they're more interested in your side of the story. Give me a statement and they'll probably leave you alone.

Bruce   Give you a 'statement'. But I haven't done anything! I can't . . . believe . . . has it really gone that far? Can't you . . . can't I just talk to them?

Robert   Well . . . not really. There's a Procedure.

Pause.

Bruce *reads.*

Bruce   'The Authority recommends that a senior consultant confers treatment with an outpatient programme.'

Robert   I think it's a good idea.

Bruce   Why?

Robert   I'm a senior consultant. He already knows me.

Bruce   What do you get out of it?

Robert   I don't 'get' anything. It's just expediency.

Bruce   'Expediency'. The Path of Least Resistance.

Robert   Absolutely.

Bruce   OK. So. You want to take over the case. And . . .

Pause.

Then you can continue Your Research?

Pause.

And Then You Can Finish Your Book. Is it a good book? It must be, you'll go to any lengths to finish it . . .

Robert   You're on very thin ice here, Flaherty.

Bruce   'The Search for the Holy Grail'.
What a chapter heading that would make.
'A Cure for Black Psychosis'.
Imagine. No more bed crises. No more hospitals.
We'd save a bundle on Care in the Community.
You'd become Professor overnight.

Robert   I *beg* your pardon!

Bruce   You heard.

Robert   Are you out of your mind?

Bruce   You'll be the toast of Academia the World Over.
Imagine! A golden opportunity to distinguish yourself from all the other boffins; To be the Eggiest Egg Head of them all; to

be *different* from all the other odious little careerists on the gravy train kissing management arse. To be Up There with all the other Cambridge wonderboys in their bow ties and tweed, flapping about the 'corridors of power' with their pricks in each other's pockets. What's wrong with just *doing your job?*

Pause.

Robert   It's the Maudsley actually.

Bruce   I'm sorry?

Robert   I read Psychiatry at the Institute of Psychiatry at the Maudsley Hospital in Dulwich. Not Cambridge.

Bruce   Oh, the Maudsley, big difference.

Robert   I really recommend you go there. I think you need to go there. And I don't mean for training.

Pause.

You're already the subject of an inquiry. If the Authority asks for a Psychiatric Report I'll be in a very awkward position.

Silence.

Bruce   OK. OK. Look . . . have you never heard . . . listen, uh, Doctor . . . did you hear Christopher refer to himself, somewhat effacingly, somewhat ironically as a, quote, 'uppity nigger'? Did you hear him say that?

Robert   It was unmistakable.

Bruce   And presumably you heard me quoting him, also, I offer, somewhat ironically?

Robert   I'd steer clear of irony if I were you. You're not Lenny Bruce.

Bruce   It was . . . it was a *nuance.* It was . . . the way I said it . . . with a note of familiarity . . . because I know him . . . and –

Robert   It's not for me to characterise your 'nuances',
Doctor. And if you ask me, yes, perhaps it was somewhat
'provocative and unorthodox'.

Bruce   Only to you.

Robert   How do you mean?

Bruce   It was provocative and unorthodox to you because,
well, frankly, it would be, wouldn't it? Perhaps you don't get
out enough.

Robert   You're doing it again: you're being provocative.

Pause.

I'm sorry, Doctor. It's pejorative whichever way you say it
and these days racial epithets just don't wash.

Bruce   'These days'. I see. Did they use to?

Pause.

Robert   You know what I mean.

Bruce *seizes the report and tears it into bits.*

Robert   May I . . . ?

He produces a mobile phone and dials.

This is Doctor Robert Smith, can somebody send
Christopher over here immediately please . . . upstairs . . . yes
. . . no, I'm in the consultation room with Doctor Flaherty . . .
no, he's my . . . no, he was but . . . he . . . n . . . I understand
but . . . well he's my patient now.

He puts the phone away.

Bruce   What did you tell him?

Robert   Bruce –

Bruce   What have you done?

Robert   It's his complaint; why don't you ask him?

Bruce   I intend to. (Just as soon as you've slithered off.)

Robert   Actually, that's not possible, I'm afraid. Not until I've briefed the patient.

Bruce   . . . What?

Robert   That's the procedure. I can't allow you to be alone with him. It's a question of Seniority as much as anything else. Perhaps if you'd shown some respect for Seniority in the first place; if you'd listened to Somebody Who Knew, we wouldn't be in this mess.

Bruce   So I'm not allowed to see Chris any more without you being present?

Robert   Anything you want to ask you must ask the Authority.

Bruce   I just *asked* 'the Authority' and I think 'the Authority' is *lying*.

Robert   I'm presenting you with the opportunity to defend yourself. That's the Procedure. What more do you want?

Bruce   Christ, it's so transparent.

Robert   Oh, do stop whining, Bruce. Before somebody nails you to a cross.

Pause.

Oh. While I'm here I should mention that I've been keeping a diary.

Bruce   A *diary*?

Robert   A diary of my research, but there are things in it which might be relevant to your case.

He produces a diary from his jacket pocket.

Now you've stopped blustering I should read you some things before my patient returns.

Bruce   You just happened to have it on you.

Robert   (*reading*)   'Twenty-sixth of October: Mention Antecedent Programme to Doctor Flaherty and he laughs.

Not interested in providing African-Caribbean and African patients for research purposes.'

Bruce I didn't laugh . . . I . . . this is silly . . .

Robert Which suggests you have been obstructive towards me from the off. I'm your *supervisor*. You don't turn down a request like that unless you have a very good reason.

Bruce I . . . look . . . I have professional reservations . . . ethical reservations about –

Robert About what?

Bruce About using patients as, as guinea pigs in, in, in –

Robert 'Guinea pigs'? Honestly, Bruce. 'Monkeys, guinea pigs, voodoo . . .' You've an entire menagerie of piccaninny slurs to unleash.

Bruce *What?*

Robert Can you not see how this could be *interpreted* – by the Authority, for example? You have to admit it doesn't look good.

Bruce Then don't show it to the Authority.

Robert I beg your pardon.

Bruce I said, don't . . . show . . . Doctor Smith . . . please . . . it's . . . it's . . . do we have to show them this?

Robert We'll pretend you didn't say that, shall we?

Silence.

Bruce *just stares.*

Robert *flips over a few pages.*

Robert 'Twenty-fourth of October: Flaherty implies research funds being used to keep me in, quote, "dickie bows and putters".'

Bruce We were *drunk*. After the rugby.

Robert *You* were drunk.

Bruce   And and and you *agreed* with me. It was a joke!

Robert   You invite me to watch the rugby with you and then you insult me. You drag me home for a chunk of rancid cheese on toast, get pissy-drunk on Bulgarian hock and start haranguing me about iniquity in the medical profession like some kind of mildly retarded student activist, then you expect the Nobel Peace Prize for Services to Psychiatry.
Why are you so threatened by my ideas?

Bruce   Because . . .

Pause.

Because they're *shit*, Doctor.
The research is banal and it's all been done before *anyway*. It's Old News. It's *R. D. Laing* in a gorilla suit.
It isn't empirical.
And it isn't a PhD.
It isn't a Book.
A *cookbook* would be more ground-breaking.
It's a waste of resources and money and everybody's time and you know it.

Robert   What are you implying?

Pause.

You see, this is just the type of verbiage –

Bruce   Verbiage?

Robert   Which people find so highly offensive about you, Bruce. This is how you wind up under investigation.

Christopher *walks in carrying a large holdall and sits down.*

Christopher   Hope I'm not interrupting.

Robert   Hello again, Christopher. I'm so sorry to send you away like that. We've concluded our meeting now and as soon as the doctor has asked you one or two more questions you'll be on your way.

Christopher   I'm going home now?

Robert   You're going home.

Christopher   Oh boy. Oh man. I'm going home.

Bruce   Chris, have I upset you in any way?

Robert   You can't ask that question.

Bruce   Why – because he might answer it?

Robert   Jurisprudence dictates.

Bruce   Are there 'charges pending'?

Robert   You are Under Investigation, yes. If there are charges to be answered then you will be suspended pending the inquiry.

Bruce   What charges?

Robert   Negligence.

Bruce   'Negligence'?

Robert   Racial harassment.

Bruce   What else? I'm intrigued.

Robert   Abuse.

Bruce   'Abuse'. Well. I was waiting for that. 'Abuse'. Mm. You know what I think? I think people abuse the term 'abuse'.

Robert   Excuse us a moment please, Christopher.

He takes **Bruce** *by the elbow and marches him to a far corner of the room.*

Robert   Doctor Flaherty, if Christopher stays in here indefinitely under a Section 3 and is diagnosed with paranoid schizophrenia, the rest of his life will be ruined.

Bruce   He won't get the help he needs without that diagnosis.

Robert   It would be negligent.

Bruce   Please, Doctor Smith, yours is an *arbitrary diagnosis*. You've observed him in one interview. It's my word against yours.

Robert   Two interviews.

Bruce   And you saw something entirely different to what I've seen.

Robert   That's the ICD 10 for you. Observation and interview.

Bruce   I think . . . look, I think he's suicidal.

Robert   He's not suicidal. He's just depressed.

Bruce   He's depressed because he's schizophrenic.

Robert   He's depressed because he's *here*. Exactly how old is Christopher?

Bruce   Twenty-four.

Robert   Twenty-four. And how do you think it feels for Christopher – a bright, fun, charismatic young man – to be locked up with chronic, dysfunctional mental patients twice his age?
People with a history of institutionalised behaviour.
People who harm themselves.
People with drug problems, who are suicidally depressed, who scream and laugh and cry routinely for no apparent reason – when they're not *catatonic*.

Have you thought about how intimidating and frightening that must be for him? Night after night after night, with no let-up.
Have you thought about what that does to a young man?
It's Like Going to Prison.
It's *cruel*.

Silence.

Now.
I have examined the patient in depth.
I have consulted with a social worker and a CPN.

Bruce   When?

Robert   In this morning's Management Hearing.
And we believe this patient will receive the treatment he
needs in the community.
We concur that the community is the right and proper place
for him.
We believe that we would be failing him by keeping him.

Bruce   So . . . it's all been settled then. I'm being overruled.

Robert   To say the fucking least, Doctor.

Bruce   So why have an inquiry.

Robert   Well, you see, for what it's worth, we're beginning
to wonder whether this patient should ever have been
sectioned in the first place.

Bruce   The, the, the police sectioned him with a 136.

Robert   Well perhaps they were being 'ethnocentric'.
He was drinking.
He was depressed.
The hospitals are full of men like Christopher.
The prisons are full of men like Christopher.
Ordinary men whose lives have flown apart and they've
found themselves in a market one day 'acting funny'. Next
day they've been locked up and a week later they're on the
coast of a crack-up. Don't you think it's time we did
something about it?

Pause.

Look at him! He's a mess. Well? What have you got to say for
yourself?

Pause.

(*To* **Christopher**.) I'm sorry, Chris.

Christopher   No, you just talk amongst yourselves. D'you
know what I mean?

Bruce *stares into space.*

Silence.

Bruce   You're not going to show me any support here, are you? As my supervisor? As a mentor? A friend?

Robert   That would be highly inappropriate.

Bruce   You've made up your mind. You support this allegation.

Robert   Not the allegation, just the inquiry. I'm afraid so.

Bruce   Golly. Just wait till I tell my wife.

Pause.

Maybe *you'd* like to tell her. Next time we invite you for dinner. Next time she slaves over a hot stove to put food in your mouth.

Robert   I'd hardly call Welsh rarebit 'slavery'.

Bruce   Next time I buy you a ticket for the rugby.

Robert   If you'd let me buy them we'd have sat in the members' stand.

Bruce   I don't even *like* fucking rugby. Bunch of hairy twats running about biting each other's ears off.

Pause.

Robert   Bruce, I'm simply asking you to give me a statement. Give the Authority your side of the story. Now. Have you got a lawyer?

Bruce   Why should *I* get a lawyer? *You* get a lawyer. *Prove* this. I can't believe this is even happening!

Robert   I really don't understand why you're taking it so personally. Why are you so angry?

Bruce   Because it *is* personal. You're somebody I trusted. I confided in. I thought you were on my side. I thought you and me could make a difference. Which is why I invited you over. My wife cooked. Nourished you. I should have choked you.

Robert   Bruce. You wanted me for your supervisor. Your mentor. You expect me to recommend your consultancy one day.

Bruce   And why did you agree – if not to get research material out of me? To finish your book. To . . . to . . . Doctor Sm . . . please . . . I don't know why . . .

Robert   I agreed because I liked you.
I thought you had promise.
I thought, such is my vanity, that you could learn something from me. Is that so difficult to believe?
Are you really so insecure?

Silence.

They stare at each other.

Christopher   You got any jelly babies?

Bruce (*to* **Christopher**)   Did I upset you yesterday? When I asked you to peel that orange?

Bruce *tosses* **Christopher** *an orange from the bowl and he catches it.*

Robert   I really don't think this is a good idea.

Bruce   Did that upset you?

Christopher *looks at* **Robert**.

Bruce   No, don't look at him, look at me.

Christopher   D'you know what I mean? I'm thirsty. I need a Coke.

Bruce   You'll get a Coke if you answer my question.

Robert   Doctor Flaherty.

Bruce   Did that upset you when you peeled the orange?

Christopher   No.

Bruce   Later, when you got to thinking about it, were you upset?

Christopher   No. It interested me.

Robert   You're pushing your luck, Flaherty.

Bruce   'No'? Oh, OK. Why do you think I asked you to peel the orange?

Christopher   To see what colour it was inside.

Bruce   And what colour was it? In your own words.
Without any help from me.

Christopher   In my own words. Blue.

Bruce   Peel another one. See if it's still blue.

Robert   I really don't recommend this.

Bruce   Go ahead, Christopher. Why not? I'll even let you
eat it.

Pause.

Christopher *peels the orange.*

Pause.

He begins eating it suspiciously.

Bruce   What colour is the orange, Chris?

Christopher   Blue.

Bruce   OK. And what do you think that means?

Pause.

Christopher   Something to do with my dad.

Robert   OK, that's enough.

Bruce   Something to do with your dad? OK.

Robert   I said –

Bruce   And what do you think I think it means?

Robert   Enough!

Bruce   What do *I* think it *represents*?

Christopher   S . . . omething to do with my dad?

Robert   This is not the time or the –

Bruce   Any idea what?

Robert   . . . Place.

Christopher   Nope. No idea, man.

Bruce   Well, I have no idea either.

Christopher   Maybe it's a signal.

Robert   . . . I must insist –

Bruce   Or a coincidence?

Christopher   No, it ain't a coincidence.

Bruce   What's it a signal of then?

Christopher *produces the crumpled newspaper cutting from his pocket and smooths it out, shows it to* **Bruce** *who shakes his head slowly.*

Christopher   Idi Amin Dada. See? '*Da-da.*' That's another signal.

Bruce   No, Chris . . . I'm sorry . . . please.

He touches **Christopher** *on the arm.*

Bruce   Put it away now. Concentrate.

Robert   Don't you think you're being a bit arbitrary?

Bruce   What?

Robert   Why should he put it away?

Bruce   'Why'?

Robert   Yes. He's not a child. Why should he?

Pause.

Bruce   Because he cut it out of the newspaper.

Robert   'Because he cu –' Really?

Pause.

And and and what makes you think that?

Robert *snatches the article from* **Christopher** *and examines it.*

Bruce   It's just a hunch.

Robert   Well, my hunch is that he didn't. My hunch is that his mother gave it to him. What is it about this particular disclosure that makes you so uncomfortable, Bruce?

Bruce   What makes me uncomfortable is that this morning he told me his father was Muhammad Ali. He'd seen him on breakfast television winning Sports Personality of the Century.

Silence.

Robert (*to* **Christopher**)   Is this true?

Christopher   1974. *Zaire. Think* about it, man.

Robert (*to* **Bruce**)   Why didn't you tell me this before?

Bruce   Before when?

Robert   Before . . . *now.*

Pause.

You told me about his mother in Feltham, blue oranges and the Chevrolet but the Rumble in the Sodding Jungle you didn't deem appropriate! Jesus wept!

Silence.

OK. Now. OK, what have we got here? One of the most feared men in history and one of the most loved. Both immensely powerful. Both role models. Both of African origins.

Christopher   Both Muslim Fundamentalists.

Bruce   Abso-fucking-lutely! Christopher, please. I want you to concentrate on the orange –

Robert   I am warning you, Doctor –

Bruce   What does it represent now?

Robert   It was stipulated at the Management Hearing that you have no further contact –

Bruce   What do you think Doctor Smith thinks it represents?

Robert   Listen . . . Christopher –

Christopher   That's easy –

Robert   Chris . . . ? Bruce –

Bruce (*to* **Robert**)   Grant me this one favour, please: listen to your patient. Chris?

Christopher   He says it's a *person*.

Robert   I never –

Bruce   A person. What kind of person?

Robert   – said anything of the –

Christopher   A Brother.

Robert   No. That's enough.

Bruce   And do you agree with that?

Christopher   I don't know.

Robert   What I said was . . . what I meant was . . . and you obviously completely misunderstood me . . . was –

Christopher   You did –

Robert   Enough! Let me finish –

Christopher   You said it was *me*.

Robert   OK, OK, OK, OK, OK, OK, OK . . . OK . . . Now . . . I commented, I merely *commented* that . . . I *suggested* that it was an unfortunate demonstration which could potentially be viewed . . . by *somebody* very vulnerable . . . by a patient . . . as an 'analogy'.

Bruce   But it wasn't an analogy.

Robert   All right . . . nevertheless . . . it could be 'taken the wrong way'. It could 'cause offence' . . .

Bruce   But it didn't cause offence –

Robert   Well . . . in hindsight –

Bruce   In whose hindsight?

Robert   OK, all right, whatever the *fucking semantics*, it was an unfortunate incident –

Bruce   It wasn't an incident –

Robert   All right, it was very, very . . . it was *upsetting*. He was upset by it, that's all and so, so, so I brought it up in the Management Hearing –

Bruce   Oh, *you* brought it up in the Management Hearing?

Robert   What?

Bruce   You said *you* brought it up. You just said that. You said you brought it up at the Management Hearing this morning.

Silence.

Christopher   And he said I should learn to lick my own balls. He did. Ridiculous but true.

They all stare at each other.

Robert *rubs his eyes.*

Christopher   (Do I look like a contortionist?)

Bruce   So . . . Doctor . . . *you* made the Complaint. *You* lodged this complaint with the Authority.

Robert   The patient was very upset. He was in no state to –

Bruce   Were you upset, Christopher?

Christopher   What? When?

Robert   He was. Take my word for it.

Bruce (*to* **Christopher**)   Are you upset now?

Robert   I'm going to go berserk in a minute. I am trying to straighten this out for you! I am trying to help.

He takes out his packet of cigarettes shakily.

(*Lighting up.*) Give you the benefit of my . . . erudition . . . and experience . . . as a Senior . . . as Senior . . . *Senior* Consultant . . . *Head* of Department . . .

Christopher *takes a cigarette and the lighter and lights it, also shakily.*

Bruce   Christopher, if I upset you, I apologise. Sincerely. I didn't mean to upset you. Did I say anything else that upset you?

Pause.

Chris?

Christopher   You put thoughts in my head.

Bruce   What kind of thoughts?

Christopher   Just thoughts.

Robert   I have to insist this stops right now.

Bruce   Shut up. Chris . . . ?

Robert   Christopher. Not another word.

Bruce   Can you think of anything specific?

Christopher *stares at* **Bruce**.
Christopher *spits the orange out and stares at the remaining segments in his hand.*

Christopher   The thoughts I have are not my thoughts. He said that I think your thoughts.

Bruce   *Doctor Smith* said?

Christopher   And that's why I have to get out of here.

Robert   That's not what I said.

Christopher   I've gotta get outta here cos of you, man!

Robert   Look . . .

Christopher   Cos you're *bad*.

Robert   OK . . . Christopher –

Christopher   And now I don't, I don't, I don't know what to think! I don't know what to think any more.

When I do think, it's not my thoughts, it's not my voice when
I talk. You tell me who I am.
Who I'm not. I don't know who I am any more!
I don't know who I am!

Robert   Chris –

Bruce   Chris –

Robert   It's being here that's doing this to you. This place –

Bruce   You're still very confused –

Robert   You can't think straight in this place. How can
you . . . ?

Bruce   You're safe here, OK? It's quiet –

Robert   Apart from the bloodcurdling screams of all the
other mental patients –

Bruce   Chris, you need to do this, you must try and stay a
little longer –

Robert   You can leave now if you want to leave now –

Bruce   Chris –

Robert   But you have to want to.

Christopher   I do want to!

Bruce   Are you sure you're ready?

Christopher   No, man, I'm not sure of anything!

Robert   Christopher –

Bruce   Chris –

Robert   Listen . . . list –

Bruce   Chris –

Robert   Chris –

Christopher   OK OK OK JUST SHUT UP JUST
SHUT THE FUCK UP FOR ONE MOMENT FOR

GOD'S SAKE YOU ARE DRIVING ME AROUND THE BEND!

Silence.

Bruce   OK, look . . . (*To* **Robert**.) Could we have a minute alone please?

Robert   Absolutely not.

Bruce   I don't think you're in a position to argue any more.

Robert   You're only making it worse.

Bruce   Nevertheless. I think you should.

Robert   OK! OK! It's *your funeral.*

Robert *exits.*

Silence.

Christopher   What the fuck do you want, Bruce?

Bruce   Well, um, well, um, I'd like you to understand that this is a very serious situation.

Christopher   Yeah, but the thing is, like he said, I don't think you should take it so personally, d'you know what I mean?

Pause.

Bruce   Well. You know. Um. I know. Yes. I'm trying.

Christopher   When somebody does something you don't like, you should just learn to laugh. D'you understand?

Bruce   Y – OK – OK. The thing is, Chris . . . see . . . I'm not very good at this. I'm not very good at . . . Not Taking Things Personally.
That's all. I like to . . . Get to the Bottom of Things.

Christopher   You don't say.

Bruce   No, I'm not being funny. Things here at the hospital, at work, I take personally sometimes. I'm ever-mindful of the way one's *professional* life impacts upon one *personally.* Just as what happens to *you* here impacts upon your personal, private life. It's all related. So you see, when you took your complaint to the Authority one of the things they concluded was that I had been 'unprofessional'. Which is in their jurisdiction to decide – they are generally more venerable – more experienced, judicious beings than I. However, the upshot is that depending on what happens now . . . I could possibly be sacked in the *first month* of my training! It isn't your fault. And I am not taking that personally. But what I would like to point out to you is that, that could well affect *both* our personal, private lives in a, in a *terrible, disastrous* way. OK? Do you understand now?

Christopher   Don't patronise me.

He eyeballs **Bruce**.

Pause.

Christopher   I had a life before this. I had a job. On a stall in the market.

Bruce   That's what I'm saying.

Christopher   I got stuff to go back to. I've got my mum.

Bruce   Your mum can't help you just now.

Christopher   She needs me. She gets lonely. I miss her.

Pause.

Bruce (*gently*)   Chris . . . you don't know where she is, do you?

Pause.

You see, my point is, when they let you out this afternoon, the theory is that you'll go back to your family. To your community. But you don't have any family, do you? Not any more. Not so far as we know. And, the thing is, should you come back, should you ever need to return and ask for my help, I might not be here.

Christopher   I'll see Doctor Smith.

Bruce   I . . . I know. But, um . . . you can see him *anyway*.

Christopher   How d'you mean?

Bruce   There's no need for you to press ahead with this complaint. If you no longer want me to treat you, I won't.

Christopher   I don't.

Bruce   Then I won't. Fine.

Christopher   Cos you put your thoughts in my head.

Bruce   OK, well . . . you know, Chris, I really didn't mean to. Maybe other people have put thoughts in your head too but they're not going to be birched for it. Do you, do you, do you see what I mean?

Christopher   No.

Bruce   I'm saying . . . look . . . I don't know what Doctor Smith said to you yesterday evening, OK, I have no idea – actually, I have a pretty good idea and I think . . . I'll be honest with you. I think Doctor Smith 'coached' you in what you had to say to the Authority.

Pause.

I think he put words in your mouth.

Christopher   He put words in my *mouth?*

Bruce   Yes. Not literally. Figuratively. OK . . . don't get excited.

Christopher   No, *you* put words in my mouth. When I said I wanted to stay and I was scared, that was you. That's why I'm here now! Cos of *you!*

Bruce   No. OK? Now . . . no. Just . . . No. Just let me read you something.

He takes a pamphlet from **Christopher**'s *file.*

I'm going to give you this to take with you. Whether you stay or go. This is what the World Health Organisation has to say about schizophrenia. I don't want to alarm you, but I want to explain to you what you've just said. I want to 'demystify'.

He reads.

'The most intimate thoughts . . . are often felt to be known or shared by others and explanatory delusions may develop, to the effect that natural or supernatural forces are at work to influence the individual's thoughts and actions in ways that are often bizarre.'
Sound familiar?

Long pause.

Christopher *snatches the pamphlet, screws it up, throws it on the floor.*

Christopher   You're just trying to get off the hook now.

Bruce   Just listen to me. You don't know what you're talking about.

Christopher   Why? Cos I'm an 'uppity nigga'?

Bruce   Look. Shut up a minute.

Christopher   Oh, that's very nice, that's lovely. It's all coming out now.

Bruce *slams his fist on the table.*

Bruce   This isn't a game! My career is on the line!

Christopher   Your 'career'?

Bruce   And your . . . your . . . you have got so much to *lose*! We both have, don't you see this?

Christopher *kisses his teeth.*

Bruce   Chris . . . please, for God's sake. Can you remember what you did in the market with the orange? Can you see how that could get you into a lot of trouble? If you were doing that . . . on the estate, for example, I don't know what could happen . . .

Christopher   I never trusted you. Mm-mm. I liked you, but I never trusted you.

Bruce   What . . . ?

Christopher   You told me I could have a Coke, yeah? In front of a witness you said I could have a Coke if I answered your questions and I answered your questions so where is it? D'you think I'm thick or something?
D'you think I'm thick?
You told me you were letting me out and now you're not. What's going on, Bruce?

Bruce   I am, Christopher, I will.

Christopher   When?

Bruce   Soon.

Christopher   Oh 'soon'.

Bruce   When you've been diagnosed properly. You must try and be patient.

Christopher   I don't *believe* you. You call me nigga. You say it's voodoo.

Bruce   It was a joke!

Christopher   Oh funny joke. Do you see me laughing?
I've got one for you. I'm gonna Lay Charges.
Cos I ain't staying here, man.
You'll never keep me locked up, white man. This is one nigga you don't get to keep, white man. Cos I'm gonna bark every time you come near. D'you understand?

Bruce   Is this you or is it . . . someone else? Is this the *illness* or is it . . .

Pause.

Maybe you're just *like* this.
Maybe you're just . . . A Wanker.
I mean . . . why do you say these things?

Christopher   Cos you ruined my life!
Cos you're Evil.
And you're a Fascist.

Bruce   How dare you!

Bruce *stands.*

Christopher *stands.*

Bruce You fucking idiot . . . What Have You *Done*?

Christopher *starts to laugh.*

Bruce What's funny? Stop laughing! Shut up! You stupid fucker. What are you laughing at?

Robert *is standing in the doorway, unseen.*

Bruce Shut up! For fuck's sake!

Christopher The look on your face, boy!

Bruce You won't be laughing when you get home. You won't be laughing when you start losing your marbles all over again and hearing voices and jabbering like a lunatic and shitting yourself because you think your fucking zombie neighbours are coming to eat your brains, you mad bastard! You *idiot*!

Christopher 'Love Thy Neighbour' it says. How can I love my neighbour when my neighbour is fascist?

Bruce They're black! All your neighbours are. It's a *black neighbourhood*. You you you *moron*. You stupid *fool*. Are you *retarded*? Jesus! This is the thanks I get for *rotting* in this stinking hellhole, pushing shit uphill, watching what I say, tiptoeing around, treading on eggshells, *kissing arse* while you sit around laughing and squawking and barking like a freak. You didn't know if you were Arthur or Martha when you came in here and this is the thanks I get. Now you're upset. *Now* I've upset you. Good. *Good*. See how much you like it.

He sees **Robert** *standing in the doorway and stares.*

Robert When you use the term 'neighbour', do you mean it rhetorically or 'generically'?

He comes into the room, takes an orange from the bowl, sits and peels it as he talks.

Because it's just occurred to me that when Chris talks about his 'neighbour', he might not mean literally 'the people next door'. Do you, Chris? Nor would you mean 'sibling' should you allude to a 'Brother'. (*Eating.*) Neighbours is Everybody, isn't it? People in the street giving you a wide berth. Women on escalators holding their handbags that little bit tighter as you pass. People looking straight through you as if you're not even there. Football hooligans. Skinheads. Throwing bananas. Your workmates. Bruce and I can only *guess* at the horror of suffering from acute paranoia *and* being one of a culturally oppressed minority. What a combination.

Pause.

And we ask each other, Why are our mental hospitals full of young men like this? Why do you *think*?

Pause.

Bruce   Robert-Robert-Robert-Robert-Robert-Robert-Robert . . .

Pause.

Doctor . . .

Robert *produces a prescription pad from his pocket and writes a prescription.*

Robert   Why don't you report to outpatients and they'll organise you a car.

Pause.

Chris? Then you can go home.

Christopher   Do you think I should?

Robert   Yes. You must.

Christopher   Do you think I'm ready? Really?

Robert   Yes. You're ready. You can't stay in here for ever. (*To* **Bruce**.) Can he?

Bruce   I . . . what . . . ?

Robert   Do you want to get better?

Christopher   Yeah . . . I want to.

Robert   Then you must do what you must do. Be brave.

Christopher   Uh?

Robert   Be brave.

Christopher   'Be brave'?

Robert   Yes. Because you are brave. You're a very brave young man and you've done really well. This is your prescription.

He hands **Christopher** *the prescription.*

Christopher   Did you hear what he said?

Bruce   I'm sorry. I didn't mean it.

Christopher   Why d'you say those things, man?

Bruce   I really am sorry.

Christopher   My God. It really is a game of two halves with you, d'you know what I mean?

Bruce   Are you all right?

Christopher   What? *No.* That *hurt*, man. I can't stay in here if you're gonna say shit like that. D'you know what I mean? Running your mouth. It's *rude*.

Bruce   I know.

Christopher   It's *weird*.

Bruce   Sure.

Christopher   How would you like it?

Bruce   I know . . . I'm sorry.

Christopher   No, you don't know. How would you like it?

Robert   If you'd like to make another complaint –

Christopher   I *am* complaining. I'm complaining to *him* and he's not even listening.

Bruce   I . . . I think I need to sit down.

Robert   Would you like to lodge a complaint with the Authority?

Christopher   No. I'm OK.

Robert   It's really no trouble.

Christopher   I'm all right now.

Bruce *sits.*
He stares.
They regard him as he picks up a piece of orange peel, examines it, bites into it.

Robert   I'll get one of the nurses to book your first outpatient appointment.

Christopher   Thanks.

Robert   Don't mention it.

Christopher   No really, safe, man. I appreciate it.

Robert   It was the least I could do.

Christopher   Thank you.

Robert *offers his hand and they shake hands.*
Bruce *just stares from one to the other.*
Christopher *goes to* **Bruce***, suddenly staring oddly.*

Silence. **Christopher** *picks up an orange.*

Christopher   Have you ever stuck your dick in one of these?

Bruce *looks at him a little nervously.*

Christopher   One time I tried it with a grapefruit. At Christmas. It's OK but it chafes a bit. The juice stings. On the ward I seen one boy do it with bugs. Straight up. Puts a bug on the end of his willy. A cockroach. Just on the tip. He likes the way it wiggles. You think there's bugs in this?

Bruce   I'm . . . sorry . . . ?

Christopher   Is there bugs in this?

Bruce   Chris . . . please . . .

Christopher   I need a girlfriend, man. D'you know what I mean? That's all I ever wanted. I just wanted somebody nice to be with. A lady.

Silence.

Robert   Take it with you if you like.

Christopher   Uh?

Robert   Take it. Be my guest.

Pause.

It's a gift. It's time to go home.

Christopher   What have you done to it?
What have you put in it?
What are you staring at?

Christopher *ignores the orange.*
He stares from **Robert** *to* **Bruce** *suspiciously.*
He moves a few steps towards the door, then stops.

Robert   That's right. Off you go. Go home and listen to some reggae music.

Christopher *stares at* **Robert** *for some time.*
Robert *eventually smiles and indicates the door.*
Christopher *goes.*
Robert *looks at* **Bruce**, *shakes his head, 'tuts' at length.*

Bruce   'Reggae music'?

Robert   What is it in Africa, 'jungle'? N'ha ha ha. (*Snorts.*)

Bruce *picks up an orange.*

Bruce   Well. That's that, then.

Robert   How do you mean 'That's that'?

Bruce   I've fucked it up, haven't I?

Robert   Oh, I see what you mean. Well . . . yes.

Bruce   I'll never make Consultant.

Robert   You still want to?

Bruce   Well . . . of course . . . but . . .

Robert   Oh.

Long silence.

Bruce   Unless . . .

Robert   What's that?

Bruce   We . . . don't really have to pursue this . . . now . . . do we?

Robert   Well, I can tell you, I'm in no hurry to have the good name of my department dragged through the mud. Thank you very much.

Bruce   No . . .

Pause.

Not to mention . . . not to mention your Professorship.

Robert   My Professorship? How does it affect that?

Bruce   Well . . . it doesn't.

He retrieves and carefully unfurls the remains of the screwed-up, torn report.

So . . . where do we go from here?

Pause.

I mean . . . what's the procedure? We were getting on quite well. Until . . . this . . . disagreement.

Robert   It's a little more than that.

Bruce   But it's . . . I mean . . . uh . . . you're a good supervisor.
And a valuable mentor.

Pause.

I'm pr . . . I'm privileged. I'm grateful to you.

Pause.

For . . . putting me straight.

Pause.

One could have made a dreadful mistake.

Pause.

Perhaps . . . I could . . . buy you a drink . . . to express my gratitude.
Debrief.
I could read your manuscript.

Pause.

Robert   No. I don't think we'll do that.

Bruce   W . . . why not?

Robert   Well. The thing is . . . I'll tell you something.

He takes the report from **Bruce** *and smoothes it out.*

Robert   I don't like you, Bruce.
You talk too much.
You get in the way.

Silence.

You see, sick people come to me.
All creeds and colours.
They are suffering.
They go away again and they no longer suffer.
Because of me.
All because of me.
And there's nothing wrong with that.
Is there?

Bruce   Who do you think you are? God?

Robert   How does Archbishop of Canterbury sound? N'ha
ha ha.
You will not be employed by this Authority again. We made
a mistake. It's a little Darwinian, I admit, nevertheless.
Goodbye.

He hands **Bruce** *the orange.*

You can eat it on the train.

Bruce *stares at the orange in his hand.*
He slumps in his chair.
He peels the orange.
He stares at **Robert***.*
Robert *goes.*

Bruce   I want to make a complaint.

Robert *stops.*

Bruce   I'd like to lodge a complaint with the Authority.

Robert   Sorry?

Bruce   I'm ready to give you a statement.
What's the procedure for that?

Bruce *bites into the orange. They stare at each other.*

Blackout.